THE SICILIAN MAFIA
A TRUE CRIME TRAVEL GUIDE

CARL RUSSO

Copyright 2013 by Carl Russo

All Rights Reserved
No part of this book may be reproduced, stored in a retrieval system, or transmitted in any form, by any means, including mechanical, electronic photocopying, recording or otherwise, without the prior written permission of the publisher, except by a reviewer, who wishes to quote brief passages in connection with a review written for inclusion in a magazine, newspaper or broadcast. Requests for permission should be directed to strategicmediabooks@gmail.com, or mailed to Permissions, Strategic Media Inc., 782 Wofford St., Rock Hill Sc 29730.

13-digit ISBN 978-1939-521-05-7
10-digit ISBN 1-9395210-5-X

CONTENTS

Introduction 5
Acknowledgements 13

PART ONE: PALERMO AND ENVIRONS **15**
1. Central Palermo 17
2. Western Palermo 45
3. Southern Palermo to Ciaculli 65
4. Bagheria to Sciara 83
5. Northern Palermo 99
6. Addaura to Mondello 107
7. Giardinello to Sagana 113
8. Piana Degli Albanesi to Camporeale 121
9. Partinico to Monreale 133
10. Castellammare Del Golfo to Capaci 141

PART TWO: CORLEONE AND THE INTERIOR **159**
11. Corleone to Mezzojuso 161
12. Bisacquino to Sutera 181

PART THREE: THE WESTERN COAST **197**
13. Salemi to Pizzolungo 199
14. Sciacca to Racalmuto 217

Bibliography 233
Index 237

INTRODUCTION

In the spring of 2006, the people of Sicily were celebrating more than the passing of another cruel winter. Italy's most-wanted Mafia chief, Bernardo Provenzano, had just been arrested after forty-three years on the run. The headlines read like pulp fiction: Mafia godfather nabbed in Corleone! Shack filled with religious icons! I happened to be traveling on the island a few weeks after Provenzano's capture. The godfather's shack: I had to see it. After two days of pestering Corleonese hoteliers and baristas, I found the small adobe hovel in the mountains above the Mafia town so celebrated in the popular culture. But tracking down just the one location wasn't enough. I also wanted to see the courtyard where the bullet-riddled body of the bandit Giuliano—chewed up and spit out by the Mafia—was laid out for carnivorous newshounds. But how would I find it? "There ought to be a book," I said. Famous last words.

TRAVEL

The purpose of this book is not to provide the traveler with tips on finding a cheap hotel or a fabulous restaurant. That information is already covered by a surfeit of travel books, websites and mobile applications. This guide is written for the adventurer interested in going beyond Sicily's amazing beaches, churches and museums. The crime buff in everyone is given a closeup view of the mysteries and savageries of Sicily's tragic past—and its hopeful future. As much as this book is a traveler's companion, it is also for the armchair voyager who may never set foot on Sicily's shores. The stories and images are presented geographically and may be read from start to finish, as narrative strains overlap and crisscross in time.

My focus is on the western half of the island, the true heart of the Sicilian Mafia. The archetypes of the village godfather, the estate enforcer, the racketeer and the hit man all have their origins in the cities of Palermo, Corleone and the surrounding country. From this rustic landscape rose the world's most infamous crime bosses, whose militias were powerful enough to wage war on the Italian state. From the northwest fishing villages and the landlocked sulphur towns came the gangsters of the American and Canadian mafias—household names to this day. The bloodiest, most tragic and literally earth-shaking events in the history of Cosa Nostra took place in the provinces explored in these pages: Palermo, Trapani, Agrigento and a portion of Caltanissetta.

This book divides western Sicily into three large sections: the metropolitan area of Palermo, Corleone and its surrounding towns and the coastal areas from Trapani to Agrigento. The numbered chapters represent car tours that may reasonably be taken in a single day. Reasonably, I posit, because car travel in

INTRODUCTION

Sicily is daunting even with the aid of a GPS device. Whether negotiating the manic traffic of Palermo, with its ancient labyrinth of streets, or the impossible Escher-like configuration of a hilltop village, much of Sicily remains uncharted by satellite street mapping. The addresses I include will, at best, only partially aid in GPS navigation. The best roadmaps are deficient—no great pity as many city streets and country roads lack signs or even a name. Let the spirit of adventure triumph over frustration.

The wisdom of traveling to some of the more trouble-plagued areas, particularly Palermo, is to be questioned, and rightfully so. It is unlikely that a typical tourist willingly strolls the grim halls of the ZEN housing projects or cares very much to see the modern Pagliarelli prison complex. In that sense, I've already made the journey and taken the photos so you don't have to. But to the irrepressible crime aficionado, these places are an essential part of the story, and some may seek them out. As in any big city, tourists should take precautions against petty crime. Purse snatches and muggings are not uncommon in Palermo and Agrigento. Your set of street smarts should be based on a few simple rules: conceal your money, stow your camera when not in use, avoid sketchy streets after dark and have an awareness of your surroundings.

My two guiding principles while "trespassing" on historical Mafia territory are *discretion* and *respect*. The emotional and ethical aspects of "Mafia tourism" come into play especially in the small villages of the interior. Almost invariably, the families of both Mafia antagonists and victims still live there. Some very awful things happened in these places and the memories are still fresh wounds. The vast majority of Sicilians are honest, law-abiding and fun to meet, but it is rude and possibly dangerous to bring up the subject of the Mafia. *Never disturb the occupants of the private homes listed in this book.* Let courtesy and common sense prevail. Overall, tourists are greeted warmly by Sicilians and they are often quite curious about you. The smaller the village, the more stares you'll receive. This should not unnerve you—a smile and a *Buongiorno!* will always be returned. Despite the language barrier, the old Sicilian-speaking pensioners of the piazza will never refuse a friendly handshake.

While I've dispensed with general travel advice, it should be noted that those who make the trek in spring will be rewarded with a dazzling display of wildflowers that cover entire hillsides in crimson, burgundy, yellow and white. The weather is pleasantly warm and the price of accommodation is reasonable. In the countryside, you're never far from an agriturismo, usually a converted farmhouse or palazzo that offers lovely rooms and local cuisine for a fair price. Whenever possible, try to patronize businesses that refuse to pay the "*pizzo*"— extortion. The growing list of anti-Mafia businesses may be found at addiopizzo.org/pizzofree.

PREHISTORY

To touch down in Palermo is to be immersed in the Mafia. The airport is called Falcone-Borsellino, named for the two anti-Mafia magistrates blown up weeks apart in 1992. The reason the airport is where it is—too far from the city and too close to the mountain—is because local Mafia bosses owned the land and steered the building contracts their way. As you drive to the city center, two ominous, rose-colored obelisks mark the spot where Giovanni Falcone, his wife and his bodyguards were blown heavenward by a stash of TNT planted under the freeway. Though diminished thanks to recent crackdowns, organized crime is still an enormous drain on the Italian economy—the abundance of trash piles is one visible consequence. Although Mafia groups

INTRODUCTION

active in other parts of Italy have grown to eclipse Cosa Nostra, almost every Sicilian town and urban district still suffer under the influence of some local crime family. This social framework goes back centuries.

Sicily's great trade advantage as a Mediterranean crossroads was also its great curse. Colonized through the millennia by innumerable foreign powers, the island's inhabitants rejected their faraway rulers as illegitimate and impotent. Many violent uprisings jolted the island after Ferdinand III consolidated the kingdoms of Naples and Sicily in 1816. This royal descendant of the Spanish branch of the Bourbons—he changed his name to Ferdinand I of Sicily—was viewed as only the latest of conquerors. In 1860, Garibaldi's forces raided Sicily and Naples, and the Bourbon regime fell. Those two consolidated kingdoms were pulled into the Italy we know today. But Sicily remained a political powder keg. Revolutionaries split into pro-unity and Sicilian autonomist camps, with Bourbon loyalists conspiring at the edges. Battles in the streets of Palermo were a common occurrence. Additionally, the sanctioned authorities of the newly incorporated region had to contend with two competing forces: unofficial roving militias and the bosses of the rural estates.

Although European feudalism was officially abolished in the eighteenth century, the Sicilian peasantry's traditional right of common land use was no better than a dependent form of sharecropping. This arrangement choked off not only the peasants' income but much of their food supply. The farms and grazing lands, owned by nobility, fed a sumptuous lifestyle in Palermo and oth-

Monument to Mafia victims: Piazza XIII Vittime, Palermo.

er cities, far from the dust of labor. From the teeming pool of landless peasants emerged what may be described as the prototypical mafioso: the *gabelloto*, a lease-holding boss. He was selected for his ability to manage the fields and quell revolts with heavy hand—that hand usually brandishing a shotgun. Many of those decadent absentee landlords lost their lands to the monsters they created. The *gabelloto* took over regulatory functions and became the de facto police. His power grew as he took control of both the estate and its workers, as well as the politicians who curried his favor for ill-gotten votes. Though illegal and frequently tyrannical, this parallel system of governance, with its own norms, laws and taxes, offered the only form of protection available to vulnerable Sicilians.

"Mafia," the buzzword of the 1860s that encapsulated both the tough-guy swagger of dandified hoodlums and the secret brotherhoods they formed, was soon applied to this new class of power brokers. Though the group modernized as it took over the cities, its original laws persist to this day: an allegiance to the organization, a code of honor and *omertà*—silence under the threat of death. Other age-old old customs linger as well. The severed head of an animal or a mutilated human corpse will show up in a conspicuous place to be read as a terrifying message. Reformed mafiosi of the twenty-first century still attest to the occasional use, with variations, of the ancient ritual of the burning saint. A new recruit's finger will be pricked and his blood then spilled onto a card bearing the picture of a saint, which is set on fire. As the initiate holds the burning image in his palm, he swears, "May my flesh be burned like this sacred image if I do not keep faith with my oath."

Fortunately, numerous mafiosi have broken their oaths to become *pentiti*, repentant witnesses for the justice system. The history of the Mafia is also the history of the anti-Mafia. Many of the persons profiled in this book died for taking a stand against Cosa Nostra. Whether agents of the law, journalists or ordinary merchants, these brave martyrs are honored by new generations of anti-Mafia activists. It is to these young fighters that I dedicate this book.

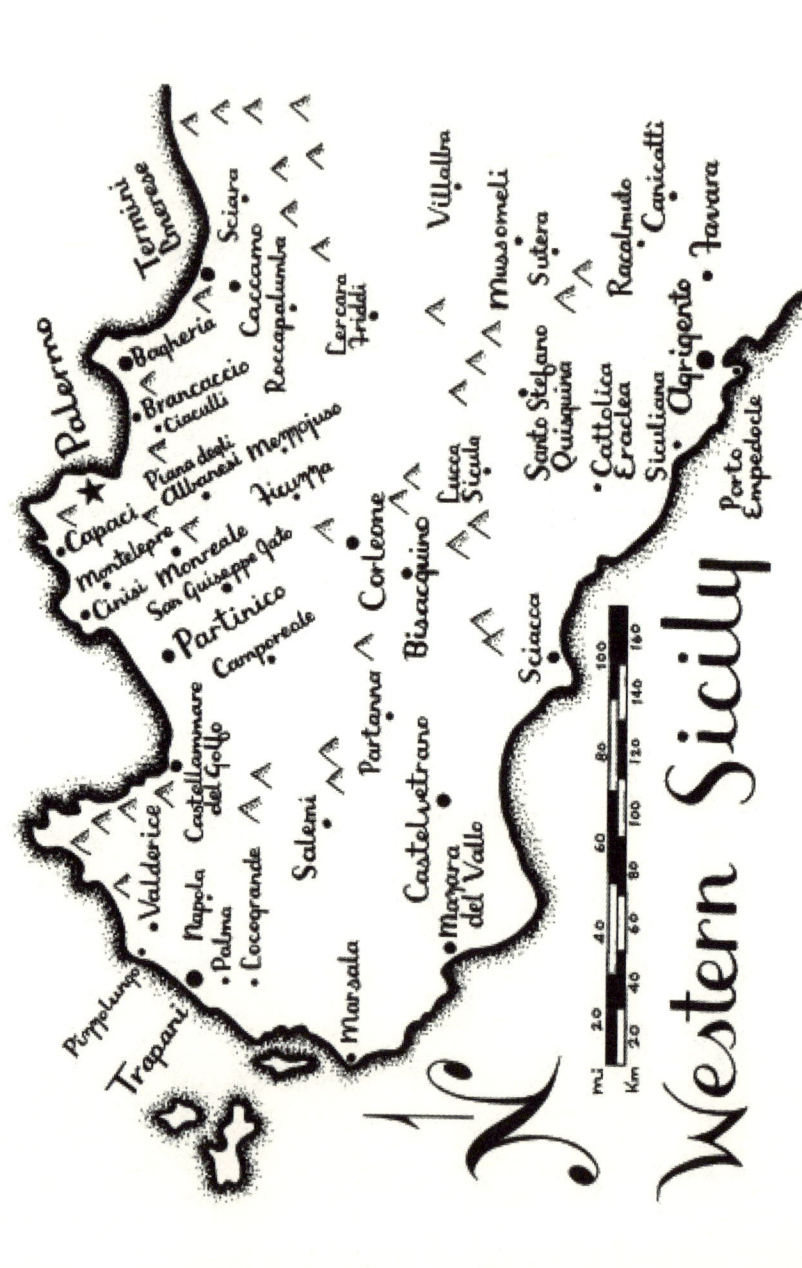

ACKNOWLEDGEMENTS

The difficult task of completing this book was made bearable by a few souls who "got" what I was trying to do. I am grateful to my publishers at Strategic Media Books, Ron Chepesiuk and Harya Dimas, for taking an interest in this project when it was still a scattered concept. I thank Crozier Green, who devised a subtitle for the book that says it all. *Mille grazie* to Gianni Aiello and David Moss for tactical support in Sicily, and to Edith J. Benay, Susan Latham and Pat Cariati for their boundless generosity. Special regards to Ronald de Grauw, who filled in the blanks with crucial photographic contributions, and to my brilliant copy editor of a sister, Susanna. Most of all, I'm thankful for the love and tolerance of Vanessa and, as always, my mother and father.

PART ONE

PALERMO AND ENVIRONS

ONE
CENTRAL PALERMO

UCCIARDONE PRISON: GRAND HOTEL

The Mafia, it can be argued, begins and ends in prison. During the tumultuous nineteenth century, a motley crowd—street toughs, town bosses and soldiers of lost causes—was cast into Sicily's dank jail cells, creating a peculiar Petri dish of hybrid criminal culture. Fittingly, King Ferdinand III's most lasting legacy is a massive stone fortress that has served as a prison since 1837. Originally called La Vicaria, its permanent name evokes the notoriety of Sing Sing or Alcatraz to Italians: Ucciardone. In 1863, the stage play *I mafiusi di la Vicaria* debuted to a smashing success and the term "Mafia" spread beyond Sicily. The plot concerned Sicilian patriotism shared by an imprisoned revolutionary lawyer and his criminal cellmates. The theme resonated with audiences—the prison populations of Sicily and Naples were known as surrogate states run by the underworld bosses confined within. Loyalty from top to bottom has remained a longstanding tradition to this day. A lowly hit man takes comfort knowing that the Mafia will protect and

The Bourbon fortress of Ucciardone has been a prison since 1837. A courtroom bunker was added in 1980 to house the Mafia maxi-trials: Via Enrico Albanese, 3.

care for his family and provide the expert legal counsel he cannot afford on his own.

Until recent laws placed stronger restrictions on detained mafiosi, life at Ucciardone was as busy—and brutal—as Mafia society outside the gates. In 1946, a black market gasoline operation was uncovered. Inmates and guards had tapped into the prison pipeline to extract the fuel, which was then sold on the outside. In the early 1950s, blankets, sheets and lightbulbs were the hot items. After two prisoners were poisoned to death in 1954, public outcry forced out the warden. He was replaced by a hardliner, whose prison inspections turned up weapons of every description. This new warden found five hundred cases of injuries caused by "falling down the stairs"—a Mafia euphemism for punishment—recorded in the infirmary files. A mutiny erupted, blessed by the mob bosses at liberty. The convicts overtook the guards and locked them up before climbing onto the roof to hang banners in support of the deposed warden. It took two days and troops from across the island to suppress the riot.

Succeeding wardens were only too happy to extend privileges to the godfathers who kept their underlings in line. This tradition of luxury behind bars for elite bosses is what earned Ucciardone the monicker of "Grand Hotel." Lobster and champagne were dropped off regularly at the admissions office for the condemned mafiosi of a 1963 police massacre. Gerlando "The Sage" Alberti lounged about in silk bathrobes, Gaetano Badalamenti flashed his solid gold watches and Pietro Torretta drew his smoke through a gem-studded silver cigarette holder. The bubbly continued to flow for Tommaso Buscetta's visitors and lawyers in the hospital suite, where he served his sentence in the 1970s for a double murder. He had an open telephone line and could prepare or order the gourmet meals of his choice. As late as 2011, there were reports of inmates sporting Armani and Gucci, a *Godfather*-style wedding in the prison chapel and a birthday feast in the gym with lobster and champagne.

Totò Riina, the feared "Beast" of Corleone, was never a clothes horse—he passed his first sentence in the frumpy field clothes of his rural past—but obeisance was paid to this boss of bosses. Prisoners passing his cell grasped his finger in tribute through the peephole and bowed their heads when he was given free movement on the grounds. The beast in Riina rose up, though, when he got word that a low-level hood in the prison badmouthed him. He sent Giuseppe Marchese, his faithful soldier, to kill the offender in his cell. The task was accomplished, in one of Ucciardone's bloodiest inside jobs, with an iron skillet. The prison added an enormous concrete bunker in 1980 to handle the prosecution of 475 suspected mafiosi. Military tanks patrolled the perimeters during these so-called maxi-trials. Defendants were led from the prison through a long tunnel, watched by armed guards, to be placed in some thirty steel cages set around the courtroom arena. This series of trials, which began in February 1986 and ran for two years, was the largest Mafia prosecution in history.

NICOLÒ TURRISI COLONNA AND THE SECT

Nicolò Turrisi Colonna, the Baron of Gorgo and Bonvicino, was a founding father of both post-revolutionary Palermo and the newly unified state of Italy. Rich in land and gifted in business acumen, the Sicilian noble was elected to the senate in 1861 and served as Palermo's mayor in the 1880s. Years earlier, when he led the National Guard across the island's lawless terrain, Turrisi Colonna noted the the presence of a secretive criminal group. A pamphlet he penned, *Public Security in Sicily in 1864*, describes a "sect that gives protection and receives assistance from certain men, . . . that has little or no fear of the public forces because it believes it can easily fly from its pursuit, that little fears judicial punishment, flattering itself with lack of evidence and the pressure that it exerts on witnesses." Though the word "Mafia" is absent, Turrisi Colonna betrays an intimate knowledge of the "sect" gained from his association with Antonino Giammona, the notorious mafioso captain of the National Guard that Turrisi Colonna himself had appointed.

In 1874, the police stormed one of Turrisi Colonna's estates and arrested three fugitive mafiosi employed there as private guards. The baron appointed his personal lawyers for their defense and sought the ouster of the prefect who had ordered the raid. As a liberal and a landholder, he condemned the harsh suppression of mafiosi as counterproductive and called for methods to modify their behavior instead. In a country plagued with ban-

Bust of Nicolò Turrisi Colonna, City Hall: Piazza Pretoria, 1 (photo: Ronald de Grauw).

dits, armed strongmen with a propensity for violence were considered a necessary evil. The basic reciprocal relationship of aristocrats like Turrisi Colonna and enforcers like Giammona has survived to the present day. An unscrupulous politician may count on the local crime boss to deliver his people's votes in exchange for favors and political immunity. Senators, governors and mayors are routinely prosecuted for Mafia association and dozens of Sicilian municipalities have been dissolved since the 1990s due to infiltration by the "sect."

JOE PETROSINO: NEW YORK'S FINEST

Joe Petrosino—born Giuseppe—was a boy when he came to America, with his father, on the first wave of Italian emigrants who arrived in the 1870s. Petrosino witnessed the birth of the New York Mafia as ethnic gangs—many Italian—carved turf out of his lower Manhattan neighborhood. He rose from street sweeper to celebrated city cop to the country's first Italian police lieutenant. His embodiment of the American Dream was a bit rough: a short bull of a man who, it was said, "knocked out more teeth than a dentist" in the course of extracting confessions. Though not a Sicilian—he was born south of Naples—Petrosino's undercover talents and knowledge of southern dialects made him the scourge of "Black Hand" extortioners and counterfeiters. Parsing the clues of a particularly brutal murder led Petrosino to suspect the dominant Morello gang of Little Italy, associated with a powerful Sicilian emigrant, godfather Vito Cascio Ferro. The NYPD was on the lookout for the capomafia as a suspect in a kidnapping, but he had already fled to New Orleans then slipped back to Sicily where he reestablished his power. Cascio Ferro was aware, in February 1909, that Petrosino was coming to Palermo on a secret mission to investigate Sicilian Mafia connections. Indeed, everyone knew as the secret had been splashed across the pages of the New York newspapers.

New York detective Joe Petrosino ate his last meal at the Caffè Oreto (left) before being shot to death across the street: Piazza Marina.

Expecting to find the same work environment he had known in New York, Petrosino refused the protection of armed police in Palermo and even left his handgun in his hotel room before dining on the night of March 12. Following his meal at the Caffè Oreto, the lieutenant crossed the street and paced the gardens of the Piazza Marina, waiting, it is believed, for someone claiming to be a confidential informer. Instead, two men with with guns arrived and shot him in the chest and neck. A final blast to the face sent his brains flying. 200,000 mourners turned out for Petrosino's funeral procession in New York. President Theodore Roosevelt, a longtime promoter of the officer, said, "I knew him for years, and he did not know the name of fear. He was a man worth while." Don Vito Cascio Ferro, roundly thought to have commissioned the murder, was never prosecuted for it. His alibi placed him in the presence of a member of Parliament at the time. The godfather remained in power in Sicily for decades to come.

THE 1957 SUMMIT: MEETING OF THE MOBS

After World War II, America's population of junkies swelled to hysteria-inducing numbers, courtesy of the New York Mafia families that pushed French-made heroin. The Narcotic Control Act, passed by the US Congress in 1956, took a sledgehammer to the illegal trade: two hundred gangsters suddenly found themselves serving forty-year prison sentences. Their brethren in Sicily, while finding it lucrative to smuggle morphine in orange crates, were still more invested in peddling contraband cigarettes. Lucky Luciano's Mafia summit of October 1957 changed all that. The Sicilian-born gangster, recently booted from America, summoned New York boss Joe Bonanno and his associates to Palermo for a four-day convention with the leaders of Cosa Nostra. All the young bloods of Sicily gathered at the luxurious Hotel des Palmes: Tommaso Buscetta, Gaetano Badalamenti and others, along with the old guard in the person of figurehead godfather Giuseppe Genco Russo. From New York, Bonanno brought along his consigliere, Carmine "Cigar" Galante, a man who would be instrumental in establishing drug routes to continental Europe, New York and Montreal. During the twelve-hour meetings, the Bonanno crime family was put in charge of the transatlantic importation of heroin from Sicily. By using Sicilian labor, operations would be off the radar in Italy, with its low rate of drug addiction. Bonanno convinced the Sicilian clans to adopt an American-style Mafia Commission to keep order in an enterprise with a fast turnover. Despite later denials by Bonanno and Buscetta that the Mafia had embraced narcotics, the heroin accord, reached at the 1957 summit, enriched mob bosses on both sides of the Atlantic and modernized Cosa Nostra.

Lucky Luciano's Mafia summit was held in the Sala Wagner (above) at the Hotel des Palmes: Via Roma, 398.

EXCELLENT CADAVERS OF 1979: CESARE TERRANOVA AND BORIS GIULIANO

Cesare Terranova cast the mold for the brilliant anti-Mafia magistrates to come. In the aftermath of the First Mafia War of 1963, the Sicilian investigator succeeded in dragging many of the biggest Mafia killers and drug traffickers to court—the so-called Trial of 114. But in the 1960s, the prosecution of a Mafia case was a radical judicial departure and Terranova watched all but a few mob bosses walk away for lack of proof in December 1968.

One of those acquitted was Luciano Leggio, vicious boss from the city of Corleone. Judge Terranova persisted. Only a few months later, Leggio was again facing Terranova in court, foaming at the mouth with hatred for the judge. Leggio played dumb, claiming he knew neither his given name nor his family's surname. The droll Terranova read into the record that the accused man "doesn't know whose son he is." The charges against Leggio and his sixty-three codefendants dated back to crimes in Corleone from the 1950s: the nine murders that cleared the way for Leggio's takeover. Witnesses at the trial were scared silent. Judge and jury alike received letters warning that any guilty verdict would result in their being "blown up" and "butchered along with your family." In the end, Leggio and his cronies—underbosses Totò Riina and Bernardo Provenzano among them—went free.

Murder site of Judge Cesare Terranova and his driver: Via Edmondo De Amicis, 7.

Few in law enforcement knew the makeup and method of Cosa Nostra like Terranova. He filled volumes with analyses of the phenomenon. Elected to Parliament in 1972, he went to Rome and served on the Anti-Mafia Commission to focus on the criminal infiltration of politics. As the influence of the Sicilian Mafia spread to Italy's capital, Terranova urged the compromised Christian Democrat party to put its house in order. But he became frustrated by the inaction of the Commission. He finished out his term and, in June 1979, returned to Palermo to fight the Mafia his way. "Don't worry," he told his wife, "they don't dare touch judges." On the morning of September 25, Terranova drove toward the Palace of Justice with his bodyguard, Lenin Mancuso, seated next to him. Turning up a side street, the car was blocked by a road barrier. Two men appeared and started firing handguns and a Winchester rifle at them. Terranova attempted to throw the car into reverse as Mancuso drew his Beretta pistol, but both men were instantly shot up. One of the assassins finished Terranova at point-blank range with two bullets in the neck. Mancuso died later in the hospital. The killing of Terranova had been approved, unanimously, by the *Cupola*, the regional Mafia Commission of bosses. Later, at his murder trial, Luciano Leggio recalled the humiliating grilling he'd received from Terranova. "If I could have bitten him then," he said, "I certainly would have poisoned him." Despite this homicidal admission, given under oath, Leggio was again set free for lack of proof.

That was the second Mafia assassination to rock central Palermo in the span of two months. The first had been that of state police chief Boris Giuliano, head of the investigative Flying Squad, who was gunned down on July 21 as he paid for his morning cappuccino at the neighborhood bar. The hit was risky as Giuliano was known to be a sure shot who carried two guns. Equipped with a wild-west mustache and FBI training, they called him "the Sheriff," but with his well-honed sleuthing skills, they might have called him "Sherlock." The killer's hand trembled as he fired twice at the officer's head and four times at his back. Like Judge Terranova, Boris Giuliano surpassed his colleagues in knowledge of the Mafia's inner sanctum. The police chief intuited a Sicilian-American heroin connection before he had any proof, eventually finding it, in the summer of 1979, on the baggage carousel of the Palermo airport: a pair of unclaimed suitcases containing half a million American dollars. The hot cash had been payment for a large package of heroin seized at New York's JFK airport. Giuliano also had a utility bill, pulled from the pocket of a detained mafioso, addressed to a house containing a hoard of evidence: nine pounds of heroin, an arsenal, a group photograph of the Corleonese Mafia and a fake driver's license belonging to Leoluca Bagarella, an enforcer for Leggio.

Police Chief Boris Giuliano was killed at the Bar Lux: Via Francesco Paolo di Blasi, 17.

With additional evidence—bank checks found on the body of a murdered boss—Chief Giuliano was able to trace billions of lire to banks controlled by Michele Sindona, the wealthy financier under US indictment for fraud. The money trail connected Sicilian traffickers to the Gambino family of New York. With the help of the US Drug Enforcement Administration, Giuliano proved that Asian heroin was being refined in Sicily for the American market. Simultaneously, Giuliano conducted an investigation into the mysterious disappearance of Mauro De Mauro, a journalist interviewed for a Francesco Rosi documentary. It was Rosi who coined the phrase "excellent cadavers" to describe those illustrious officials assassinated by the Mafia. The murders of Terranova and Giuliano—two men who had embodied excellence—were part of a now regular pattern.

EXCELLENT CADAVERS OF 1980: PIERSANTI MATTARELLA AND GAETANO COSTA

Sicilian governor Piersanti Mattarella was killed in his car on the way to Mass: Viale della Libertà, 147.

As a member of an opposition party, Judge Cesare Terranova's attempt to rid the Christian Democrats (DC) of Mafia infestation had been a vain attempt. Piersanti Mattarella, a loyal DC politician, was better positioned to delouse the party. Not only had he come of age in the centrist fraternity, he was also the son of Bernardo Mattarella, a high party chieftain whom Joe Bonanno considered his host during the gangster's visit in 1957. Piersanti Mattarella upset the party in 1976 by running an alternative slate of candidates to compete with the underhanded delegates behind the so-called Sack of Palermo, the Mafia's wholesale redevelopment of the city. Although his faction lost, Mattarella was elected as governor of Sicily two years later, a win that jeopardized the sweet relationship the DC enjoyed with the Mafia. Mattarella passed a series of laws tightening the regulation of public contracts—measures that ended decades of fraudulent disbursements and single-bid graft. He also made moves to attract clean investments from northern Europe, which would further weaken Cosa Nostra.

Ignoring the death threats he received by telephone, Mattarella relieved his bodyguard for the day on Sunday, January 6, 1980. The governor drove with his wife to Mass and had stopped near the church when a man strode up to the car aiming a pistol at him. Mattarella's wife screamed and pleaded for her husband's life. But the man grinned perversely and fired, killing Mattarella as his wife watched in horror. Palermo grieved at this latest assassination. Amid the dignitaries who filed past Mattarella's body, lying in state in his office, were ordinary citizens—baby strollers and all. Under the sway of boss Stefano Bontate, the offing had been ordered by the Mafia Commission. It came as no surprise to the Christian Democrats' top brass in Rome. Party leader Giulio Andreotti initially met with Bontate but he could not save the life of the reform-minded Mattarella. The parliamentarian learned the high price of his party's rapport with the Mafia. Afterwards, Bontate reportedly threatened Andreotti with the words, "We're in charge here in Sicily, and if you don't want to destroy the DC, you'll do what we say."

Another "excellent cadaver" turned up in May 1980 in the neighboring town of Monreale. The murder of carabiniere captain Emanuele Basile provoked an aggressive police response: fifty-five mafiosi were picked up on drug charges. Chief among them was Rosario Spatola, a boss of the powerful Inzerillo family. A farcical courtroom showdown between head prosecutor Gaetano Costa and two of his examiners nearly scuttled the case. Costa's assistant prosecutors, having promised the Ma-

Prosecutor Gaetano Costa was assassinated while browsing books: Via Camillo Conte di Cavour, 161.

fia's lawyers the speedy release of their clients, sparred with him over procedure—one even refusing to honor the arrest warrants. Rather than allow Palermo's worst malefactors to slip through his fingers, Costa signed new warrants for the lot. He also reopened a homicide case against trafficker Gaetano Badalamenti. On the scorching afternoon of August 6, Costa stood browsing the used books of a sidewalk stall. A driver in a Fiat A112 screeched up and a gunman jumped out. He pumped three .38-caliber bullets into Costa—two in the back and one in the head—then sped away on the seat of a Honda scooter, driven by a third accomplice. Costa quickly bled to death on the ground. Two days earlier, police had found Totuccio Inzerillo loitering near Costa's home, but the Mafia boss was not detained. The Costa case was never solved.

CARLO ALBERTO DALLA CHIESA: FLYING SOLO

To Carlo Alberto Dalla Chiesa, accepting another assignment in Sicily was like stepping back into battle. A decorated brigadier general of the carabiniere—the militarized state police—and a hero of Italy's anti-terror initiatives of the 1970s, Dalla Chiesa was publicized as the government's best weapon against the Mafia. It was his third stint in Sicily and his last chance to take down the gangsters he'd been fighting since the 1940s. He had already conducted a career's worth of Mafia investigations, but on his return in 1982, the organization was a bigger, bloodthirstier creature. On his first day of duty, the general attended the funeral of Pio La Torre, a deputy who had tried unsuccessfully to pass laws expanding the powers of anti-Mafia prosecutors. The government in Rome was happy to bestow the title of Prefect of Palermo on Dalla Chiesa, but it was loathe to grant him the full authority he needed to go after the backers of Cosa Nostra. His personnel was a skeleton crew.

Despite receiving letters of support from average Sicilians, Dalla Chiesa felt isolated and doomed. Refusing bodyguards and armored vehicles to keep a fleet-footed step ahead of the enemy, he

General Carlo Alberto Dalla Chiesa was ambushed and killed with his wife and bodyguard: Via Isidoro Carini, 34.

braved the streets of Palermo alone. He ordered roadblocks, examined bank records and spoke openly to the press. In response, he was attacked on every front. One day, an unidentified man rang the office of the carabiniere near a roadblock and announced the start of "Operation Carlo Alberto." The voice alerted the agents to a car parked outside containing a pair of stiffs in the trunk. Giulio Andreotti, the leader of the Christian Democrat party, then published an editorial discrediting Dalla Chiesa as prefect. The mayor of Palermo, who was close to Andreotti, publicly condemned Dalla Chiesa's "criminalization" of his city. Dalla Chiesa was reminded of the time Andreotti had gone "white in the face" when he mentioned the Mafia crimes of the politician's Sicilian associates.

On the last day of his life, September 3, 1982, Dalla Chiesa made dinner reservations. Once a widower with a son, he had just remarried. A bodyguard driving an armored Alfa Romeo followed the couple in their unremarkable Lancia toward the restaurant. Suddenly, a motorcyclist pulled up transporting hit man Pino "Little Shoe" Greco, armed with a Kalashnikov. He led an army of seven executioners bearing more AK-47s. Little

Shoe fired at the bodyguard's car while Dalla Chiesa leapt across his wife to protect her. But another shooter killed them both, firing repeatedly into their faces. The bodyguard died later that night. Dalla Chiesa had lasted four months in Palermo before being terminated by the Mafia. Only then did Rome pass the laws Dalla Chiesa had desperately sought. In 2002, a court convicted bosses Totò Riina, Bernardo Provenzano, Michele Greco, Bernardo Brusca and many others for the massacre.

ROCCO CHINNICI: NO PARKING

Murder site of Calogero Zucchetto, a member of Chinnici's anti-Mafia pool (see Page 195): Via Emanuele Notarbartolo at Via Marchese Ugo.

During his brief tenure at the Palace of Justice, Rocco Chinnici laid the groundwork for an unprecedented series of Mafia indictments. His promotion to chief prosecutor came in 1979, a time when the Mafia was at the height of its power and the depths of its treachery. Not only had its dark angel, Totò Riina, eliminated good men like Chinnici's predecessor, Cesare Terranova, and investigator Boris Giuliano, the period was marked by the apathy and obstructionism of the Italian justice system. To match the mob in strength and wit, Chinnici assembled an anti-Mafia pool made up of the bravest and brightest public servants in his sphere. Magistrates Giovanni Falcone and Paolo Borsellino, denied even a computer by their superiors in Rome, compiled a paper mountain of illicit banking evidence. Chief Investigator Ninni Cassarà uncovered the history of heroin trafficker Michele "the

Pope" Greco with the help of able Mobile Squad agents Beppe Montana and Calogero Zucchetto. This crack team of prosecutors scored high arrest numbers and collaborated with the FBI on international cases. Following the 1982 assassination of General Dalla Chiesa, Chinnici signed arrest warrants for Greco, Riina and other gangsters behind the craven act and handed them to Falcone—a bold strike sure to provoke the bosses of Cosa Nostra.

Restaurant workers chat in front of Judge Rocco Chinnici's residence, where he and three others were massacred: Via Giuseppe Federico Pipitone, 59.

Although these agents never traveled without an armed escort, Falcone was worried about an exposed curb in front of Chinnici's condominium, recommending a no-parking zone. But Chinnici brushed off the suggestion, preferring to avoid the wrath of his neighbors.

On the morning of July 29, 1983, Chinnici left his family's apartment for the office. The concierge opened the lobby door to the street for him, as always. There, Falcone's driver—on loan while Chinnici's was on vacation—stood by with two other bodyguards at the prosecutor's armored Alfa Romeo Alfetta. Parked directly in front of the building's entrance was a nondescript little Fiat 126. As Chinnici passed it, a shockwave blew the men and the cars three stories high. Body parts, rubble and asphalt flew everywhere. A black crater three feet deep replaced the spot occupied by the TNT-laden Fiat just seconds before. Chinnici and two of his men died along with the concierge. Forty others were injured, including two babies pulled from the rubble by their parents. The armored Alfetta spared the life of the substitute driver, but the explosion caused him permanent injuries. The Mafia got its revenge for Greco's arrest warrant. Munitions expert Giovanni "the Pig" Brusca had rigged the Fiat and Nino Madonia had pushed the button. Nineteen men were involved, but the conspiracy may have stretched beyond Sicily. Two weeks before the assassination, a Lebanese morphine supplier had spilled the revenge plot to authorities. Yet no one lifted a finger to protect Chinnici and his men.

GIOVANNI FALCONE: TOO DANGEROUS TO LIVE

Judge Giovanni Falcone memorial in the Kalsa neighborhood of his youth. He played soccer here: Piazza Magione.

Giovanni Falcone had a death premonition because death was all around him. When he moved up the ladder from bankruptcy cases to Mafia prosecutions in 1979, the Palace of Justice was still reeling from the assassination of Judge Cesare Terranova, followed by that of Police Chief Boris Giuliano. Giovanni Falcone, the "super-judge" who had transformed the Italian justice system from a revolving door for criminals into an aggressive punisher, openly acknowledged he would be taken out by the Mafia. Falcone's boss Rocco Chinnici shared the same premonition and advised Falcone to keep a diary until his own fateful day. He took that

CENTRAL PALERMO

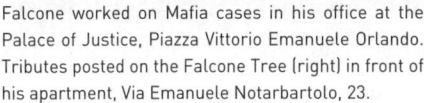

Falcone worked on Mafia cases in his office at the Palace of Justice, Piazza Vittorio Emanuele Orlando. Tributes posted on the Falcone Tree (right) in front of his apartment, Via Emanuele Notarbartolo, 23.

advice and charged ahead with the greatest Mafia indictment in history: the 1986-87 maxi-trials of 475 members of Cosa Nostra.

Falcone's ability to coax confessions from powerful Mafia bosses—much of our knowledge of the group comes from his interviews with supergrass Tommaso Buscetta—created enemies on both sides of the law. Early in his career, Falcone had shrugged off two brushes with death during prison visits: he was taken hostage at a jailhouse riot in Trapani and nearly shot in Palermo's notorious Ucciardone. But it was the bomb planted at a rented vacation house, a location known only to a few in his circle, that profoundly rattled him. Paolo Borsellino was not among the passel of Falcone's jealous superiors and colleagues in the prosecution office. The friendship Falcone shared with his fellow magistrate stretched beyond their university days and back to the ancient Kalsa quarter of central Palermo, where, as young boys, they kicked soccer balls around the piazza. Together, under Rocco Chinnici, Falcone and Borsellino built a professional anti-Mafia pool from scratch, tracing the global network of the Sicilian-American drug cartel previously hidden in the shadows of silent conspiracy.

Falcone's frustration brewed, however, as professional betrayals stacked up, from the scores of Mafia acquittals by Judge Corrado "the Sentence Killer" Carnevale to being taken off anti-Mafia investigations in later years. So, when Falcone accepted an invitation in early 1992 to head up the Penal Affairs department in Rome, many thought he was taking the easy way out of a failed career. But just as he had revolutionized the prosecutorial arm of the Italian government, the "super-judge" shook up its prison system. "I was completely wrong," admitted one magistrate. "Although we were slow to recognize it, the Mafia understood right away that [Falcone] was much, much more dangerous in Rome than remaining in Palermo." Falcone's fated assassination came on May 23, 1992 (see Page 154).

PAOLO BORSELLINO AND THE VIA D'AMELIO MASSACRE

One day in that terrible Palermo summer of 1992, already darkened by the recent killing of Judge Falcone, two magistrates entered upon a scene that deepened their despair. Their colleague Paolo Borsellino sat at his desk in the prosecutor's office, head in hands and crying repeatedly, "A friend has betrayed me." Such behavior was disturbing for the heroic public servant who, as Falcone's right-hand investigator in the maxi-trials, had helped to clap the irons on nineteen powerful Mafia bosses for good. Borsellino's breakdown came from more than just exhaustion of working day and night to find his partner's killers. He had been telling everyone, "I'm looking directly at the Mafia. I have so much work to do." His work was cut short only a few days later. On July 19, Borsellino drove from his villa in a suburb to a modern apartment complex in Palermo, led and followed by the two other cars of his escort team, to fetch his mother for an appointment with her cardiologist.

The police convoy entered the cul-de-sac of Via Mariano D'Amelio, where its three drivers went into their familiar defensive positions. Borsellino parked his Fiat Croma, stepped out, lit a cigarette and smiled enig-

Paolo Borsellino's childhood home, Via della Vetriera, 57.

matically. His bodyguards moved to surround him in the well-practiced "human turtle" formation they used to move the judge through public spaces. At that instant, a great fireball exploded, piercing the quiet evening and flinging their cars into the air. A column of thick black smoke rose and obscured severed limbs jettisoned several stories high. People rushing to the scene discovered the horror of the latest Mafia attack: Paolo Borsellino and five of his escorts blown up less than two months after Judge Falcone met the same fiery fate. "I felt crushed inside and tossed around," recalled Antonio Vullo, the lone surviving bodyguard. "I didn't know what to do and I started to run. Then I saw shreds of flesh. I was standing on the foot of a colleague." Before the explosion, Vullo had been aghast by the number of parked cars that should have been removed before Borsellino's arrival. One, a Fiat 126 abandoned the day before, was packed with more than two hundred pounds of TNT. Had the compound detonated before Borsellino stepped from his armored vehicle, he might have survived as Vullo had. The judge's personal effects remained on the back seat: a singed leather briefcase containing keys, cigarettes and a still-wet pair of swimming trunks. But one important item was missing: the red notebook.

Everyone in Borsellino's circle knew about his red notebook.

He was forever filling its pages with investigative details and memoirs in his race against the clock. His wife Agnese had seen him pack it into his briefcase before leaving the villa that day, but shortly after the bombing, it vanished. Among the first to arrive at the inferno was Borsellino's friend and fellow magistrate Giuseppe Ayala. He tripped over the charred human torso, stripped of its limbs, that was once Borsellino. In 1998, Ayala, now a senator, testified that he and a policeman discovered the briefcase in Borsellino's car and together removed the red notebook. When that officer attempted to hand it to Ayala he claimed to have refused it. This was contradicted by Captain Giovanni Arcangioli, the policeman at the scene who was later charged with its theft but acquitted. Other witnesses reported differing accounts of the notebook. Adding to the mystery was the presence of a stranger, caught on film, who wandered authoritatively amid the smoking wreckage and burnt corpses.

A coalition of activists headed by Judge Borsellino's brother

Borsellino's name appears with those of other Mafia victims on the steps of Piazza della Memoria, behind the Palace of Justice. An olive tree marks the spot (right) where a car bomb killed Borsellino and five escorts in front of his mother's apartment. Via Mariano D'Amelio, 18.

Salvatore grew around the missing item as it related to the death plot. This group was encouraged by numerous revelations that emerged about an alleged agreement between the Mafia and the state that would end assassinations like Borsellino's. In 2009, the judge's widow told a court that her husband had "learned a few days before that Cosa Nostra wanted to kill him." She testified to his mistrust of a pair of carabiniere special agents: Colonel Mario Mori and Captain Giuseppe De Donno. Those men and scores more—from the lowliest Mafia soldiers to the highest politicians—became fixtures in a series of trials over supposed negotiations between the Mafia and the state. The labyrinthine proceedings brought about several indictments, convictions, sentences, appeals and acquittals. In May 2013, a new trial prosecuted ex-Interior Minister Nicola Mancino and then-jailed ex-Senator Marcello Dell'Utri for their alleged involvement in this devil's pact. Informer Gaspare Spatuzza, the Mafia killer who stole the Fiat 126 used as the car bomb at Via d'Amelio, testified to the details. The entire affair can be reduced to a single burning question: were magistrates Falcone and Borsellino killed because certain representatives of the Italian government reneged on a deal they made with the Mafia?

L'ORA: SCANDAL SHEET

The wealthy Florio family began publishing the Palermo daily newspaper *L'Ora* in 1900 to advance its business agenda. *L'Ora* quickly evolved into the leading cosmopolitan journal of the city. Luigi Pirandello and Giovanni Verga were among the men of letters who graced its pages. The Fascists shut the paper down in the 1920s but later resumed publication to promote Mussolini's colonial ambitions. Only after Italy's liberation did *L'Ora* regain

The offices of the *L'Ora* weathered a Mafia bomb attack in 1958. Piazzetta Francesco Napoli, 5.

its independent voice. The editorship moved steadily leftward with each change of hands until 1954, when it came under the aegis of the Communist Party. Reborn as a splashy modern daily, the new *L'Ora*, despite an anti-American slant, was far from doctrinaire. Its pictorials of scantily clad beauties were balanced by extensive arts coverage—author Leonardo Sciascia joined the stable—as well as hardcore investigative journalism. Three of *L'Ora*'s best reporters were killed for writing about the Mafia: Mauro De Mauro, Cosimo Cristina and Giovanni Spampinato.

Reportage of Cosa Nostra began in 1958 with inquiries into the presence of godfather Giuseppe Genco Russo in the halls of the Sicilian government and the takeover of the Corleonese Mafia by Luciano Leggio. "DANGEROUS!" read the front-page headline over a large photograph of Leggio, followed by an invitation to examine the "bloody career" of the fugitive who is "rich, feared and fearsome . . . with a pistol under his American jacket." After a subsequent issue led with the screamer, "Luciano Leggio was in Palermo," an eleven-pound charge of TNT blew up half the the printing room. Two days later, *L'Ora* was back on the stands with a note from the editor: "The Mafia threatens us, the investigation continues." Indeed, the exposés continued until the farewell issue of 1992. A short-lived revival in 2000 collapsed when the new owner was convicted of fraudulent bankruptcy. The historic offices were sold in 2004.

THE ANTI-MAFIA MOVEMENT

In southern Italy, paying the *pizzo*—or *pizzu*, in Sicilian—can feel like the natural order of things. The nineteenth-century grain farmers who turned over most of the harvest to overlords were expected to give an additional scoop, the *pizzo*, or beakful, to the estate guards. Thus, "wetting the beak" became the tribute paid to intermediaries—the mafiosi who guaranteed distant landlords a smooth operation. The long tradition of the racketeer wetting his beak by dipping into a shopkeeper's profits continues to this day. The legendary capomafia of the early twentieth century, Vito Cascio Ferro, considered the *pizzo* an integral part of Sicilian society and to be handled with care: "You've got to skim the cream off the milk without breaking the bottle," he cautioned. "Don't ruin people with absurd demands for money. Offer your protection instead. Help them prosper in business and they'll not only be happy to pay the

Libero Grassi paid with his life for refusing the pizzo: Via Vittorio Alfieri.

pizzu but they'll kiss your hands in gratitude." (Claire Sterling, *Octopus: The Long Reach of the International Sicilian Mafia*. [New York: Touchstone, 1990].) Cascio Ferro's rosy view, however, belies the nasty consequences that "ruin" can entail.

Typically, a middleman—one known to back up his authority with violence, if necessary—was given a cut of the sales transaction he was asked to mediate. A buyer was guaranteed to receive his money's worth and the seller was guaranteed to be paid. This happy arrangement became the preferred method for both buyer and seller. One sociologist famously argued that *protection* is the sole defining feature of the Mafia: "This is what distinguishes them from simple criminals, simple entrepreneurs, or criminal entrepreneurs. . . . What does make [one] a mafioso is the fact that he is capable of protecting himself as well as others against cheats and competitors." (Diego Gambetta, *The Sicilian Mafia: The Business of Private Protection*. [Cambridge, Massachusetts: Harvard University Press, 1993].) Protection as a service has devolved over time into base extortion. It thrives in Sicily precisely because it sprang from a legitimatized system. The *pizzo* is brazenly collected from grocery stores, restaurants, hotels, car dealerships, funeral parlors and even holy festivals. A retailer opening a new shop is greeted by a friendly *esattore*, a "tax collector," sent by the dominant crime family of the territory. A relationship is established based on the regular hand-to-hand exchange of cash payments. This hidden tax on Italian businesses amounts to billions of dollars annually.

Refusing to comply is risky. An uncooperative business is likely to suffer a series of intimidations that increase in severity. Its padlocks may be filled with super-glue or a small fire may be set near its entrance. A sack left at the door might contain bullets or the severed head of a goat. Arsonists often torch the owner's car, business or home. Ultimately, death can come to a refusenik. Libero Grassi, a textile manufacturer, was one of the first merchants to take a public stand against the *pizzo*. He paid with his life in 1991, but his murder inspired a wave of activism never before seen in Italy. Groups like Addiopizzo—"Goodbye *pizzo*"— launched campaigns to help businesses stand up to the Mafia. Addiopizzo was a plaintiff in the prosecution of powerful Palermo boss Salvatore Lo Piccolo. New laws have put pressure on the merchants, too, making it a crime to pay a racketeer. Sicilian newspapers still regularly detail the threats and attacks on businesses by extortioners. Despite the greater profits reaped from gambling, drugs and raiding the public till, the Mafia still keeps its beak dripping wet.

Counterclockwise from top left: Davide Grassi took over his murdered brother Libero's textile factory, Sigma Nuova: Via Croce Rossa, 238. Vincenzo Conticello, owner of the popular Antica Focacceria San Francesco, identified his would-be extortioners in court, then opened two more restaurants in Rome: Via Paternostro, 58. After losing a warehouse to arson, hardware wholesaler Rodolfo Guajana built a new one, with help from the state: Via Pietro Nenni, 14. Fabio Messina's Emporio Pizzo Free sells food products and wine made without Mafia interference: Corso Vittorio Emanuele, 172. The activist group Libera Terra sells anti-Mafia products upstairs and holds events and meetings downstairs: Piazza Castelnuovo, 13.

TWO
WESTERN PALERMO

PIETRO SCAGLIONE: SECRETS AND LIES?

On the morning of May 5, 1971, at headquarters in Palermo, the police received an anonymous call: "A shooting has happened in Via dei Cipressi. Maybe two are dead." Within minutes, the Flying Squad pulled into the cypress-lined road leading to

Controversial prosecutor Pietro Scaglione was ambushed after a visit to his wife's grave: Via dei Cipressi.

the Cemetery of the Cappuccini. A state car blocked the entrance of the necropolis, pockmarked with bullet holes. Two bodies were pulled out and rushed to the hospital, but it was too late. When the frightful news spread that Pietro Scaglione, Palermo's chief public prosecutor, had been killed along with his driver, many observers confirmed their suspicion that he was connected to the mob. At the time, the Mafia was only murdering its own. But Judge Scaglione tended to delay Mafia indictments. Palermo's police chief accused him of letting capomafia Luciano Leggio slip through his fingers, and often he had to be goaded into prosecuting a case. This inaction landed him in the hot seat before the Anti-Mafia Commission. Scaglione denied a host of charges. The Commission declared him innocent, but with a proviso: he could resume his duties as a chief prosecutor but he would have to leave Sicily and take his post in the mainland city of Lecce. So, why had Scaglione been murdered on that spring morning after making his daily visit to his wife's grave? And who was responsible?

The answer to the second question is rather established, despite the fact that no one has ever been convicted for the double murder. Three Mafia turncoats independently pointed to Leggio and laid out the scenario: as Scaglione and his driver departed from the cemetery in a state-issued Fiat 1300, another car entered the narrow Via dei Cipressi to cut it off. At the wheel was killer Pino "Little Shoe" Greco accompanied by, depending on the account, Totò Riina or another mafioso. Luciano Leggio himself fired at Scaglione and his driver from the backseat. Speculation about the motive persists. During his 43-year-career, Scaglione got about as close to the Mafia as a lawman can. He wrote down the words of the bandit Gaspare Pisciotta the night before he was poisoned to death in jail. The judge was also one of the last of Mauro De Mauro's interviews before the Mafia journalist disappeared. Plagued by relentless slander, Scaglione's murder left a stain on his life's work for years. But an attempt to redeem his reputation largely succeeded when officials, activists and historians lined up to defend him, pointing to his transfer to Lecce as proof of his valued service to the state. But was the transfer a promotion or a was it a demotion that followed his humiliating appearance before the Anti-Mafia Commission? Apparently, he had enough dirt on the Mafia to get himself killed.

THE CEMETERY OF THE CAPPUCCINI

Clockwise from top: Both Judge Pietro Scaglione and Deputy Pio La Torre were killed by the Mafia. Mayor Vito Ciancimino died in Rome at the age of 78 (photo: Ronald de Grauw). Piazza Cappuccini.

VITO IEVOLELLA: DEATH IN THE PIAZZA

When small-time Palermo smuggler Matteo Biondo went missing in the summer of 1980, his wife snooped around and discovered his harrowing demise: Biondo had been shot to bits by his business partners and fed to pigs. The desperate mother of six showed up at the office of the carabiniere to tell everything she knew to Marshal Vito Ievolella, a much-lauded anti-Mafia investigator. Signora Biondo supplied missing pieces to Ievolella's investigations into the contraband empire of Palermo godfather Tommaso Spadaro. The marshal produced a report identifying forty-five mafiosi involved in cigarette smuggling,

Marshal Vito Ievolella was shot to death in his car: Piazza Principe di Camporeale.

drug trafficking and murder—all with connections to Spadaro. This same boss took revenge exactly one year after the widow had presented her blistering evidence. On September 10, 1981, as Ievolella and his wife sat in a car waiting for their daughter to finish a driving lesson, three bullets fired in rapid succession entered his head. He fell onto his wife bleeding as a team of gunmen shot up the car. He was hit three more times and died but his wife escaped serious injury. The commandos stepped cooly into a waiting car and disappeared. Based on the later testimony of turned gangsters, Spadaro got a life sentence for the murder of Ievolella. In 2010, the boss received a degree in philosophy after completing his thesis, "Nonviolence and Gandhi's Principles of Religion."

PIO LA TORRE: BEFORE HIS TIME

Pio La Torre's radical trajectory, from peasant land reformer to parliamentarian in Rome, was driven by his lifelong desire to beat the Mafia. The Communist Party chief assisted Palermo judge Cesare Terranova on the Anti-Mafia Commission, but their investigations were mostly ignored. After Terranova was killed, an enraged La Torre proposed to renew a series of measures once enacted by Mussolini but later abandoned. If passed, individuals could be prosecuted for association with a criminal syndicate even in the absence of a criminal act. These laws could pull in corrupt politicians and confiscate money and assets gained by illicit means. But La Torre's ideas were too hot for Parliament and the legislation failed to pass. The defeat did not slow his work. According to his wife, he was also investigating a Mafia network that connected a pair of bankers with Propaganda Due (P2), a secret Masonic lodge made up of high-level statesmen and military officers.

Parliamentarian Pio La Torre and his driver Rosario Di Salvo were killed by machine gunfire: Via Vincenzo Li Muli, 3

La Torre started carrying a pistol, though the left-handed politician didn't know how to use it, and he took a different route every day on his commute to party headquarters. On April 30, 1982, as his driver Rosario Di Salvo turned up a narrow street, the two were ambushed by masked men on motorcycles. The car was sprayed by submachine gunfire, killing La Torre instantly. Di Salvo fired back with his pistol but was fatally struck seconds later. Like his esteemed boss, Di Salvo had never learned how to use a gun. On the May Day funerals of La Torre and Di Salvo, the boulevards of downtown Palermo were festooned with red banners. Crowds of angry workers assaulted the political dignitaries assembled on the dais with shouts of "You'll pay for this!" and "Which of you is the assassin?" A confidante would later reveal that the hit had been ordered by Totò Riina. Never before had the capomafia targeted a member of Parliament. But even with the horror of this double assassination that claimed one of its own, Parliament idled another six months before enacting La Torre's laws.

MAURO DE MAURO: DOUBLE SCOOP

Watched by his daughter from the family's apartment above, journalist Mauro De Mauro drove off to his doom: Viale delle Magnolie, 58.

Everything about Mauro De Mauro was an enigma, right down to the conspicuous bump on his nose. His background as a Fascist commander in Nazi-occupied Rome made him an odd fit when he took a job as a reporter for *L'Ora*, Palermo's popular left-wing newspaper, in 1959. Yet he thrived on the crime beat, filing reports that struck the Mafia like bombshells. As early as 1962, he published an accurate map of the city's clans—names and all. Informer Tommaso Buscetta said that De Mauro became "a walking corpse." "I have a scoop that will shake Italy," he told a colleague before leaving the newsroom for the night. Like any hardboiled hack from the movies, he stopped to pick up a few packs of filterless cigarettes, a bottle of bourbon and some coffee on his way home. As he parked his BMW, his daughter Franca watched him from the window of the family's apartment above. It was September 16, 1970—the eve of her wedding. Franca saw two men approach her father on the street. After exchanging words with them, he hopped back into his car and drove off. It was found the next morning, on the other side of Palermo, with the key still in the ignition. De Mauro has been missing ever since.

Official inquiries into De Mauro's disappearance relied on the accounts of Buscetta and several other repentant mafiosi and have settled on two hypotheses. The first attributes the reporter's probe of the mysterious airplane crash, in 1962, that claimed the life of Enrico Mattei, the president of Italy's state petroleum consortium. The controversial magnate had ties to the Mafia—his associate was a best man at godfather Giuseppe Di Cristina's wedding—and was at odds with the world's major oil powers. De Mauro revived his investigation for a film about Mattei in 1970. Decades later, evidence surfaced that the airplane had carried a planted bomb. A second theory about De Mauro's death, endorsed by several of the informers, involves Prince Junio Valerio Borghese. Borghese had been De Mauro's superior in a wartime unit that hunted and killed Italian partisans. But in 1970, the journalist was developing a scoop about the "Borghese coup." The prince was readying a neo-Fascist plot to overthrow the government, with the help of the Mafia, for that December. The putsch flopped, but not before De Mauro vanished. Buscetta and the others claimed De Mauro knew too much and was strangled and buried near the Oreto river. Of the numbers of bodies the police have dug from its banks, none match De Mauro's DNA.

THE CAPTURE OF TOTÒ THE BEAST

In January 1992, Salvatore "Totò" Riina "went crazy," according to a court document, after four hundred of his fellow "men of honor" were sentenced during Palermo's Mafia maxi-trials. The two chief investigators on the case, Giovanni Falcone and Paolo Borsellino, were blown to bits on Riina's orders. Likewise, crooked state officials Salvo Lima and Ignazio Salvo were gunned down for failing to intervene on behalf of the Mafia. Assassinations of this caliber, ordered by a boss without the consent of the ruling Mafia Commission, destroyed tradition and shocked

Police forced capomafia Totò Riina to a stop in Piazza Albert Einstein.

its members. At just over five feet, two inches, Riina was commonly referred to as "the Short One" by his cohorts but came to be called "the Beast" by his rivals and victims. He and his violent mentor from the old country, Luciano Leggio, drew on their experience working for Palermitan drug traffickers. Soon, they built their own heroin refineries and forged a new empire. By the early 1970s, the Corleonese bosses were rich. To take control of Cosa Nostra, Riina cozied up to certain crime families and extinguished others. He was especially adept at sowing confusion and paranoia among them, fomenting bloodbaths while appearing uninvolved. In 1974, when Leggio was caught and sentenced for the 1958 slaying of his old boss Michele Navarra, the city of Palermo passed into Riina's hands.

Riina's criminal career came to an unceremonious close nearly twenty years later. On January 15, 1993, the capomafia was being driven around the Piazza Einstein, a freeway interchange in the Uditore district, when police cars sided up to his modest Citröen and forced it to stop. Riina professed his innocence and surrendered a false ID. One officer grabbed him by the neck while another pushed his driver to the ground. As the mafiosi were taken to police headquarters, Riina—choking in a tightly wound scarf gripped by a cop—asked the identity of their captors. When they told him, he was relieved to know that the ambush was not a Mafia attack and finally admitted, "Yes, I'm Riina. Bravo.

Congratulations." Less than twenty-four hours had passed since police had discovered his hideout among a complex of luxury villas in Uditore. The carabiniere surveilled a particular house swarming with mafiosi. A reformed mafioso threatened by Riina identified three figures on the video screen as the boss's wife, son and gardener. The agents could scarcely believe their luck: Sicily's most-wanted man of the late twentieth century was theirs for the taking.

Despite the hoopla over Riina's arrest, the Italian government gleaned little Mafia intelligence from it. Police neglected to search his villa until it was too late. Within days, persons unseen stripped the house of furnishings and painted over fingerprints. Artworks and furs went up in smoke. It was later revealed that Riina's landlord had provided a perfect cover: he was the son of a famous anti-Mafia senator. Over the years, speculation grew that Riina had been betrayed. Questions and accusations swirled around Riina's freedom of movement during his long residency in Uditore. How had he been able to marry in a church with three presiding priests, one of whom was defrocked over a Mafia kidnapping? How could his wife have given birth to three of four children in a private clinic, each receiving full-name certificates and official baptisms? What about the couple's honeymoon in Venice? Whether the state was complicit or incompetent, two hundred fugitives—including "the Beast"—had roamed freely in the 1980s.

The fugitive Riina lived with his family in the luxury villa behind this gate: Via Gian Lorenzo Bernini, 54.

THE VIALE LAZIO MASSACRE

A new building stands on the site of the deadly Mafia gunfight: Viale Lazio, 106.

Reminiscent of the Saint Valentine's Day massacre of Chicago, a significant event in Cosa Nostra history occurred in 1969. As in Al Capone's Prohibition-era slaughter, six hit men, dressed as police officers, attacked a meeting in session at a construction office on Viale Lazio. Their target was Michele "the Cobra" Cavataio, an undisciplined hood who had ignited a Mafia war six years earlier by blowing up the villa of boss Salvatore Greco. To protect himself, Cavataio started blabbing about a map he had drawn that identified the entire Mafia hierarchy containing many names yet unknown to the police. The map had been a bad idea. The Viale Lazio massacre was a Palermo-Corleone joint effort. Bernardo Provenzano burst into the office shooting. The victims returned fire, killing Calogero Bagarella, the brother of Totò Riina's fiancée. While Cavataio crouched on the floor, Provenzano tried to search his body for the map. Cavataio sprung his signature Colt Cobra. Click. It was out of bullets. Provenzano grabbed his own automatic Beretta but it jammed, so he clubbed Cavataio with it instead and smashed his cranium. Then, using a pistol, he fired a bullet into Cavataio's brain. No map was ever found. It had been ripped up and thrown into a waste basket moments earlier.

DON VITO CIANCIMINO AND THE DEAL

Many questions about the late politician Vito Ciancimino have been asked, but few have been answered. Was he mafioso? Did he try to strike a deal to end Mafia assassinations? But one certainty is that Ciancimino was very, very rich. As Palermo's assessor of public works, he opened the government purse to Mafia-connected speculators during the "Sack of Palermo." Don Vito Ciancimino stood at the very vertex of organized crime and politics, taking every advantage of his position. As the middle-class son of a tradesman in Corleone, Ciancimino grew up with the Mafia. The accountancy student who tutored the younger Bernardo Provenzano in math joked, years later, that he could call the capomafia a *cornuto* and still live. In 1950, Ciancimino won a State Railways concession based on a letter of recommendation from his "political godfather," Bernardo Mattarella, a Christian Democrat dogged for years by accusations of Mafia association. Similar rumors spread about Ciancimino upon his election as mayor of Palermo in 1970. Falling under investigation for embezzlement, he stepped down after twelve days in office. But he continued to pull strings from his penthouse on Via Sciuti, the nerve center of his secret empire, where bundles of bank records were stashed under the kitchen tiles. It was here that the arrogant

The penthouse was the nerve center of Don Vito Ciancimino's secret empire: Via Giuseppe Sciuti, 85/R.

entrepreneur received Totò Riina while still in pajamas.

Nothing would stick to Don Vito until 1984, when he would be was arrested after Tommaso Buscetta told the Anti-Mafia Commission that the ex-mayor was "in the hands of the Corleonesi." Caught and released numerous times, he finally went to prison in December 1992—the first politician in Italy to be convicted for consorting with Cosa Nostra. But prosecutors didn't know the half of it. The country had been thrown into a state of shock that year with the assassinations of former mayor Lima and Sicily's top anti-Mafia magistrates, Falcone and Borsellino. Ciancimino, shaken, commented, "It's terrorism, not Mafia." In the space between the judges' deaths, June 1992, Ciancimino is reported to have become the mediator in negotiations between representatives of the government and the Mafia.

A curious story of intrigue commences with Colonel Mario Mori and Captain Giuseppe De Donno, two agents of the carabiniere's Special Operations Group (ROS), who attempted to "dialogue with the enemy." The officers recruited Don Vito in an effort to stop Totò Riina's killing spree. He then became the go-between, secretly meeting with the officers then with godfather Bernardo Provenzano and "Signor Franco"—a mysterious adviser connected to Italy's Secret Services. Mafioso neurologist Antonino Cinà then sent a document to Ciancimino that became the MacGuffin of the tale: the so-called *papello*—Riina's list of twelve conditions necessary to effect a ceasefire. These included demands to lessen prison terms inflicted on mafiosi at the maxi-trials. The purported meetings with the ROS officers took place at Ciancimino's apartment on the Piazza di Spagna in Rome. Hoping to restore the Mafia to its traditional role as a covert player, Provenzano is said to have leaked Riina's whereabouts. This allowed the ROS to capture the fugitive psycho-boss.

Such an unholy alliance between the Mafia and the state would seem outlandish if it hadn't come from the mouth of Don Vito's son Massimo, the "postman" in the negotiations, backed by the sworn testimony of several key players on both sides of the law.

CIANCIMINO JUNIOR: SINS OF THE FATHER

The Palermo residence of Don Vito's son Massimo Ciancimino was found to have thirteen sticks of dynamite in the garden: Via Torrearsa, 5.

"Crude, self-absorbed and domineering" is how Massimo Ciancimino remembers his father, Don Vito. The Mafia tycoon slapped around this youngest of his children, punishing his misdeeds with confinement in a storeroom for days, once tying him up with a chain just long enough to reach the toilet. Although his father called him "Dick-head" into adulthood, "Ciancimino Junior" remained his loyal secretary, a lackey as willing to cater to the hypochondriac's fears as to arrange his meetings with dangerous bosses of Cosa Nostra. After the death of Don Vito in 2002, Massimo was investigated for money laundering. And as the inheritor of Don Vito's "treasure"—hidden bank accounts and interests across Europe—he was made to answer for his father's crimes. An endless series of police interrogations, arraignments, house arrests and jail sentences followed. Massimo mostly cooperated, surrendering piles of his father's documents and memoirs. The findings spilled over into the parallel trials of Colonel Mario Mori and Senator Marcello Dell'Utri, the latter accused of being Silvio Berlusconi's liaison with the Mafia.

A week spent in a cell at Ucciardone prison and a new wife induced Massimo to cooperate with the state. In February 2008, he astonished his questioners by mentioning Totò Riina's *papello*. It was Massimo to whom ROS officers Mori and De Donno made an overture toward a Mafia-state deal in 1992. And it was Massimo who had couriered the sealed envelope containing Riina's demands, unopened, to his father. The son's declarations gave credence to ex-mafioso Giovanni Brusca's testimony as to the existence of Riina's *papello*. Although the ROS agents denied everything, Massimo gave investigators an earful of his father's secrets, like mucky details linking Dell'Utri and Berlusconi to the reputed deal. Massimo's cooperation ultimately lessened his jail sentence.

Massimo, now a newly minted informer, moved with his family and his state-appointed bodyguards to Bologna. In 2009, he received a sack full of AK-47 bullets and a letter threatening his little son Vito. More jail time came in 2010 after he moved back to his permanent residence, an opulent ground-floor flat in a palazzo in Palermo. Police soon discovered a 9mm pistol in the house and thirteen sticks of dynamite in the garden—enough to blow up the building. It was for his own protection, Massimo explained, after the threats in Bologna. Despite Ciancimino Junior's mafioso approach to life, his rehabilitation was generally accepted by the anti-Mafia movement. Salvatore Borsellino, brother of the slain judge, appeared with Junior on his book tour. The volume is a tell-all about Don Vito that screams with revelations—and filial revenge: "I'd pay a lot to be able to tell him, 'You can stick it, Papà.'"

THE CARABINIERE MASSACRE OF 1983

Captain Mario D'Aleo of the carabiniere unit in Monreale spent the better part of his days investigating the Mafia of nearby San Giuseppe Jato. The Roman-born careerist, still in his twenties, had stepped into the boots of Captain Emanuele Basile, assassinated by the Mafia. Without missing a beat, Basile continued his predecessor's investigation of the patriarch Bernardo Brusca's shady interests. "Be careful, because you insist on persecuting our family too much," threatened the boss's aged father. Bernardo's son Giovanni Brusca bore the brunt of the officer's diligence: he was put into the barracks on more than one occasion for questioning. One day, Captain D'Aleo and Lance Corporal Giuseppe Bommarito, a Sicilian native in his thirties who had worked alongside Basile, surprised a group of mafiosi in meeting. The presence of a Monreale boss close to the Bruscas led the officers to believe that a string of unsolved murders in the area—including that of Basile—was traceable to these men. But the investigation came to an abrupt halt.

Captain Mario D'Aleo and two agents were ambushed in front of his girlfriend's apartment: Via Cristofaro Scobar, 22.

On the evening of June 13, 1983, D'Aleo and Bommarito were being driven by a soldier, Pietro Morici, in a Fiat Ritmo patrol car—D'Aleo was to be dropped at his girlfriend's apartment in Palermo. As the Ritmo pulled up to her residence, a Fiat 131 advanced slowly toward them from the opposite direction and stopped, blocking the carabinieri. Two men leapt from the 131 firing guns from each hand. D'Aleo and Bommarito bounded from the Ritmo but were instantly mowed down. Morici died behind the wheel. None of the victims had been able to pull their guns from the holsters. The killers jumped back into the 131 and tore off. A series of hearings on the massacre began in the late 1990s featuring several detained mafiosi—some recalcitrant, others self-confessed—including Giovanni Brusca, Gaspare Mutolo, Francesco Marino Mannoia and Calogero Ganci. Ganci took the stand, where he revealed the operation had mostly been a family affair. He described how his father, boss Raffaele, met Brusca at the butcher shop that served as the contact point near the scene. From there, they drove to Ganci's grandmother's, where they had stored the firearms. The team was rounded out by his brother and his cousin.

Two facts emerged from this corroborative testimony. The first was motive, as summed up by a conspirator: "They killed this captain because he was interested in the Brusca family. Because at the time it was said that he harassed them, that he was investigating them, and, in the same way they did it to Captain Basile, they did it to Captain D'Aleo." The second fact was Mafia culpability. "D'Aleo was a captain of the carabiniere," Ganci told the court, "and I can tell you that when there is a murder of people in law enforcement, it's a decision of the [Mafia] Commission." By the time the trials wrapped in 2007, Giovanni Brusca was acquitted of the triple homicide but several others were convicted and sentenced: the hit men and their bosses, and, for "moral complicity," the entire Mafia Commission.

TOTUCCIO INZERILLO AND THE SECOND MAFIA WAR

For all the power the Corleonesi had accumulated in the 1970s, they lacked one advantage held by the rival Inzerillo family: relatives in the New York Mafia. Salvatore "Totuccio" Inzerillo, boss of Palermo's large Passo di Rigano quarter, was an in-law of the dominant Gambino family of Cherry Hill, New Jersey. Members of this extended clan included original architects of the Sicilian-American drug pipeline. Intermarriage between old and new world families produced the kind of loyal personnel required by international clandestine operations. It also gave the Inzerillos a place of refuge when the Corleonesi turned their weapons against them. Totuccio Inzerillo's compound in Passo di Rigano became the thrumming center of the Sicilian heroin trade, good for $600 million a year in US export. His son-in-law Rosario Spatola laundered profits through construction projects run by Palermo's development czar, Vito Ciancimino. Gaetano Costa, the city's chief prosecutor, was on Spatola's scent, but that was the least of the drug traffickers' problems.

Palermo boss Totuccio Inzerillo's compound was the thrumming center of the Sicilian heroin trade: Via Castellana, 346.

During this time, Totò Riina was steadily building a coalition of Sicilian bosses loyal to his Corleonese mob while simultaneously attacking Inzerillo and his allies: Stefano Bontate, who controlled southern Palermo, Gaetano Badalamenti of Cinisi and Giuseppe Di Cristina, a boss of Caltanissetta who had warned police of an imminent Mafia war. Di Cristina survived a murder attempt in 1977 but lost two of his allies to Corleonese bullets. When Di Cristina retaliated by killing a Riina-faithful from Caltanissetta, he turned up dead—provocatively close to Inzerillo's home. Such unsanctioned hits on another boss's turf are a breach of Mafia code. Inzerillo upped the ante by having prosecutor Costa assassinated in August 1980, without any approval of the Mafia Commission. The act erased the threat of Costa's investigations, but it was really meant to check Riina's dictatorial aspirations.

This newly dubbed Second Mafia War was practically a one-sided annihilation. Riina's masterful battle strategies often left the impression that his enemies were behind the bloodshed. Two hundred men linked to the Inzerillo and Bontate families were killed or went missing. Much of the firepower was supplied by Pino Greco, a terror with his Kalashnikov, and the demented Filippo Marchese. In April 1981, Greco knocked off Stefano Bontate. A few weeks later, as Totuccio Inzerillo was leaving his girlfriend's house, Greco trained his Kalashnikov on him and blasted away. Inzerillo's bulletproof car, newly purchased in fear of this moment, was parked only a few feet away. Two of Inzerillo's brothers were eliminated as well. Then Inzerillo's seventeen-year-old son Giuseppe, who had sworn to kill Riina in vengeance, was kidnapped then shot in the head by Greco—but not before he chopped off the boy's killing arm. The Gambinos flew in from America to broker a ceasefire. Riina agreed to allow the surviving Inzerillos to live in exile in New York.

Totuccio Inzerillo was killed on this spot, a few feet from his new bulletproof car: Via Filippo Brunelleschi, 15.

After a life sentence took Riina out of circulation, in 1993, various Inzerillos gravitated back to Palermo. Totuccio's American-born son Giovanni moved into the family estate in Passo di Rigano. It didn't take long for the authorities to realize that the transatlantic clan was reviving the glory days of the narco-trade. In 2008, a joint US-Italian intelligence action called Operation Old Bridge dashed their plans, rounding up ninety mafiosi in New York and Sicily. One young Palermo boss escaping capture was Gianni Nicchi.

GIANNI NICCHI AND NINO ROTOLO: MURDER LESSON

Gianni Nicchi's career in crime was meteoric as he rose from neighborhood barista to Italy's second-most-wanted mafioso by the age of twenty-seven. Devoted service to his honorary godfather, boss Nino Rotolo, included a diplomatic mission to New York to meet with the Gambinos. Upon his return, he spooked Rotolo with the news that the Inzerillo family was attempting a Sicilian homecoming, with the blessing of Palermo boss Salvatore Lo Piccolo. Rotolo personally had strangled one of the Inzerillo brothers. If Lo Piccolo allowed the family to return, there surely would be a settling of scores. A trusted deputy under Bernardo Provenzano, Rotolo killed for the Corleonesi in the war that drove the defeated Inzerillos out of Sicily. To survive, he would have to take out the Lo Piccolos, both father and son. Rotolo assigned the job to Gianni Nicchi and gave him a murder lesson. Though under house arrest, Rotolo still conducted Mafia business in a cheap shed of corrugated metal behind his luxurious villa. But the shed was bugged so the police heard everything.

"Always fire two or three shots," he instructed Nicchi. "When he falls to the ground, a shot to the head is enough. You'll see that the head makes a mess." Rotolo recommended waterproof nylon clothing, surgical gloves and a little bag of garden fertilizer to erase the telltale gunpowder burns from his arm. In the mean time, Rotolo would obtain the barrels of acid needed to disappear the Lo Piccolos literally. But this plan fell apart. In June 2006, a few months after police arrested Provenzano, Rotolo was grabbed in Operation Gotha with fifty-two other mafiosi, including Franco Bonura and Antonino Cinà. Nicchi inherited Rotolo's kingdom, centered in the Pagliarelli quarter. But the enmity between Nicchi and his foes flared the following summer with the shooting death of his business partner, Nicola Ingarao. According to two of the assassins who later collaborated with the police, Sandro Lo Piccolo was at the scene and possibly even pulled the trigger. The war ended five months later with the swift incarceration of the Lo Piccolos, confirming Nicchi as the king of Palermo's underworld. But the police were quick on his trail, too. On December 9, 2009, he was traced to a downtown apartment just blocks from the Palace of Justice. He was thrown in the Pagliarelli prison complex located in the heart of his own home turf. In 2013, Nicchi was sentenced to ten years.

Boss Nino Rotolo conducted business in a shed behind his villa (left), while police listened in: Viale Michelangelo, 450. His successor, Gianni Nicchi, was captured on the second floor of a villa: Via Filippo Juvara, 25.

THREE

SOUTHERN PALERMO TO CIACULLI

STEFANO BONTATE, THE PRINCE OF VILLAGRAZIA

Francesco Marino Mannoia, a skilled chemist with a Midas touch for refining heroin, became a precious witness for state prosecutors when he decided to talk in 1989. As the first member of the Corleonese mob to break ranks, he revealed a Mafia web that entangled politicians, industrialists and even the Vatican. One name he invoked often was that of his ex-boss Stefano Bontate, the drug lord who reigned over the Santa Maria del Gesù quarter of Palermo. Bontate, known as "the Prince of Villagrazia"—so named for the long street on which he lived—was a dashing scion of an old Mafia family. His father, the formidable Don Paulino Bontà, a pallbearer at the funeral of the historic godfather Calogero Vizzini, had been powerful enough to slap a member of the Sicilian parliament without consequence. Bontate the younger, however, had to remake himself after the Mafia War of 1963 reduced him to a cigarette smuggler. But his supply route was readily adaptable to heroin distribution and he became a principal trafficker in partnership with Totuccio Inzerillo and the Gambinos of New York.

Drug lord Stefano Bontate met with politician Salvo Lima at the Baby Luna bar on closed days. Behind the Mafia hangout was one of the Inzerillo-Bontate group's many heroin refineries: Viale Regione Siciliana Sud Est, 1843.

Both Marino Mannoia and Tommaso Buscetta told investigators that Bontate had been involved in a series of crimes, such as the strange disappearance of journalist Mauro De Mauro and the phony disappearance of "God's Banker," Michele Sindona, a financier flush with Vatican and Mafia money until a stock market crash wiped him out. According to Marino Mannoia, Sindona reinvested the Inzerillo-Bontate group's profits and staged his own kidnapping in a bizarre blackmail ploy to recover lost money. It was a spectacular failure that ended with Sindona convicted of murder then choking to death on cyanide in prison. The Sindona affair also exposed P2—Propaganda Due—a defunct Masonic lodge reconstituted in the 1960s as a right-wing shadow-state run by political and corporate luminaries. Bontate's Masonic lodge mates in Sicily formed a tight circle of "friends" that included the Salvo cousins and the Sicilian politician Salvo Lima, a member of Prime Minister Andreotti's cabinet in Rome.

It's not surprising that the Corleonesi, who could not abide competing power, turned against the politically juiced Bontate and Inzerillo. While both men were members of the Mafia Commission, Riina kept them in the dark about the assassinations he personally ordered, provoking Bontate to threaten him. The Second Mafia War was declared on April 23, 1981, with Stefano Bontate's murder. The boss, driving home in his Alfa Romeo following the celebration of his forty-third birthday, came to a stop

Stefano Bontate lived at Via Villagrazia, 151, just down the street from his younger brother Giovanni, at 173-183. Both men were killed by the Corleonesi in the 1980s. (Photos: Ronald de Grauw.)

at an intersection in his neighborhood. Pino Greco and a team of hired guns were ready for him. A few weeks later, it was Totuccio Inzerillo's turn to get it. Giovanni Bontate, Stefano's younger brother and a key operative in the family business, resisted the pull to take over as top boss—yet he was also killed, in 1988. With the competition out of the way, the Mafia's country cousins from Corleone could be said to have conquered Palermo.

PAGLIARELLI PRISON: SUICIDE ROW

When the soldiers of most-wanted kingpin Salvatore Lo Piccolo were marched into Pagliarelli prison following his 2007 bust, the inmates from the rival province of Trapani burst into song praising their fugitive leader, Matteo Messina Denaro. The taunt turned to applause and signaled, to some, the loss of Palermitan superiority. Whatever the significance, the new Mafia had a new prison: Casa Circondariale Pagliarelli, named for the neighborhood it dominates. The complex was completed in 1991 to house thirteen hundred inmates, with a separate wing for women. Its cellblocks have hosted bosses like Gianni Nicchi, Mafia affiliates like Massimo Ciancimino and former Secret Services agent Bruno Contrada. A tougher prison combined

Pagliarelli: the new Mafia got a new prison. Via Vittorio Bachelet, 56.

with tougher sentences made inside killings more difficult at Pagliarelli. Suicide in the general population, however, was apparently epidemic. There were eleven in 2012 alone and the prison police said they stopped more than two thousand during the previous two years. News of the 2008 suicide of mafioso Gaetano Lo Presti was exceptional for its rarity in the Mafia's culture of extreme machismo. Despite having just completed a twenty-seven-year sentence, police tapped his telephone and got an earful of useful information that prompted their roundup of ninety-four suspected mafiosi. Lo Presti was sent to Pagliarelli. The boss was also heard crowing about his ascendency in the organization thanks to the backing of Salvuccio Riina, son of Totò "the Beast." When Riina Junior was picked up as a result, Lo Presti knew he was a dead man. He formalized his status with a noose in his cell.

FILIPPO MARCHESE'S ROOM OF DEATH

Corso dei Mille runs along Palermo's southern waterfront. The boulevard is named for Garibaldi's thousand-soldier advance on the route in 1860. That era's splendor of palaces and citrus groves was replaced with reckless development and gridlocked traffic, the very air tinted orange with smog. In the 1970s, the decaying neighborhood was ruled by one of the Mafia's most degenerate bosses, Filippo Marchese. He operated his own rackets and was implicated as a drug trafficker who laundered earnings through the banks. But he also played a significant role as an executioner for the Corleonese Mafia, led by Totò Riina. Marchese set up a grisly death factory in a filthy, abandoned apartment near the shore called the Room of Death. His victims were generally the losers of the Mafia war of the early 1980s, hoodlums who ran afoul of the Corleonesi.

Degenerate boss Filippo Marchese set up a grisly death factory, near the shore, called the Room of Death: Via Ponte di Mare.

Interrogations in the Room of Death were conducted at a table set with a few chairs. While a crew of four or five men restrained a victim with ropes or chains, Marchese took personal pleasure in doing the strangling himself. Other times he snorted cocaine and masturbated to the spectacle.

One crew member who did not relish the killings was Vincenzo Sinagra, a dimwitted young man compelled to do the boss's dirty work on pain of death. Dishonored after getting caught stealing from a Mafia affiliate, Sinagra's servitude included the kidnapping and delivery of victims to Marchese, holding their feet as they struggled, dissolving the dead bodies in a barrel of sulfuric acid and sometimes dumping into the sea whichever body parts had not melted. The twisted Marchese, who actually crossed himself before he committed murder, once chastised Sinagra for looking horrified during a routine strangulation. Lethal revenge was always the modus operandi of the Corso dei Mille family. After a massacre of enemy mafiosi in nearby Bagheria—an act ordered by the Corleonesi—a set of bloody fingerprints found at the scene was traced to Filippo's nephew Giuseppe Marchese by Professor Paulo Giaccone, director of forensic medicine at Policlinico hospital. Though pressured by a

Mafia-connected colleague to "soften" his conclusion in favor of the nephew, Dr. Giaccone refused. Within the year, he was shot dead on hospital grounds. Today that hospital is named in Giaccone's honor. According to an informer, the logic of Mafia justice applied to Filippo Marchese as well, and after he had outlived his usefulness to Totò Riina, he too was chopped up and dissolved in a barrel of acid.

Counterclockwise from top: Vincenzo Sinagra dumped undissolved body parts into the sea: Caletta Sant'Erasmo. Policlinico hospital is named in honor of Dr. Giaccone: Via del Vespro, 127. Five bullets through a heart mark the spot where Giaccone was killed: Policlinico campus.

LEOLUCA BAGARELLA: FAMILY MAN

From May to July of 1993, Cosa Nostra exported its terror to the great cities of northern Italy. Its first attack, a car bomb in Rome, coincided with a meeting of the Anti-Mafia Commission on the first anniversary of Judge Falcone's assassination. One week later, a bomb exploded near the Uffizi Galleries in Florence, killing four people and destroying priceless paintings at the Georgofili Academy. Another bomb at the Palazzo Chigi, the prime minister's residence in Rome, was defused on the anniversary of the Italian Republic. Yet another, near Milan's Gallery of Modern Art, killed three firemen and a police officer. Still more bombs ripped apart sections of the centuries-old walls of two Roman churches: San Giovanni in Laterano, where ten people were killed, and San Giorgio in Velabro. This mass destruction was Totò Riina's response to Article 41b, Italy's tough anti-Mafia measures enacted the year before. To accomplish such difficult feats, he relied on Leoluca Bagarella, the clan's savage hit man who was also his brother-in-law. Though not a mastermind, Bagarella was able to pull off the bombings with the loyal Graviano brothers of southern Palermo and Matteo Messina Denaro, the up-and-coming boss of Trapani.

One of Leoluca Bagarella's former residences, according to court records: Corso dei Mille, 742.

Bagarella was a pedigreed mafioso, kid brother to tough Calogero, who was one third of the old Corleone triumvirate with Luciano Leggio and Riina before perishing in the Viale Lazio massacre. Bagarella proved his mettle by taking out Palermo police chief Boris Giuliano and had emerged as a frontline killer with Pino Greco during the 1979-80 Mafia war that erased a thousand enemies. After nabbing Riina in 1993, police considered Bagarella his heir apparent. Though a practitioner of quick hits and slow strangulations, Bagarella was a devoted husband who craved the life of the traditional "man of honor"—he even used the *Godfather* theme on his wedding video. But his wife lost a succession of babies to infant death, perceiving their bad fortune as punishment for Bagarella's kidnapping of twelve-year-old Giuseppe Di Matteo. She also suffered the humiliation of seeing her mafioso brother cooperating with the judicial system. Following a number of failed suicide attempts, she eventually hung herself at home. The fugitive Bagarella had to carry her body out for a secret burial. After the police tracked him down in 1995, they entered his home and discovered fresh flowers set before a picture of his wife on their wedding day.

THE GRAVIANOS: BLOOD BROTHERS

The Graviano brothers kept apartments on permanent reserve at the San Paolo Palace Hotel, part of their illicit business empire: Via Messina Marine, 91.

A sophisticated investigation of Riina's bombings of continental landmarks led to two mafiosi at the scene in Florence: Giuseppe and Filippo Graviano. The aggressive, enterprising bosses from Brancaccio were trusted allies of the Corleonesi. The brothers' close proximity to the territory of the conniving boss Michele Greco, a co-head on the Mafia Commission, comforted godfather Totò Riina. The Gravianos were active players in Riina's plot to kill both Falcone and Borsellino in 1992. Henchman Gaspare Spatuzza called Giuseppe Graviano "Mother Nature"—an unstoppable force. The Gravianos kept apartments on permanent reserve at the San Paolo Palace, a hotel they owned on the waterfront, just north of

Brancaccio. This holding was just part of an empire that included land, homes, stores, bars, gas stations and betting rooms. After the brothers were caught in 1994, the San Paolo was confiscated by the state. But as late as 2011, the bellboy at this "symbol of the anti-Mafia" was actually believed to be a mafioso who had inherited the Brancaccio territory from the Gravianos. At the time, the San Paolo was registered in the name of Gianni Ienna, a rich builder who was also frontman for the brothers. Ienna used the hotel to host a support club for Silvio Berlusconi's Forza Italia party.

But the siblings made good use of their jail time. They embarked on self-improvement regimens that earned Giuseppe a degree in mathematics and Filippo one in economics. Their Web-savvy sister Nunzia was put in charge of the family investments. The 1999 arrests of some Graviano affiliates brought charges that their $6,000-a-month attorney had arranged illegal conjugal visits, allowing the bosses to father children while still in prison. The Gravianos landed back in court in 2011 to fight off Spatuzza's allegation that they had had secret dealings with Prime Minister Berlusconi. But despite the world notoriety of their political assassinations, the Gravianos are best remembered for ordering the death of a humble Catholic priest in Brancaccio.

BRANCACCIO

PINO PUGLISI: BLESSED BALL BREAKER

The name of Father Giuseppe "Pino" Puglisi is forever associated with Brancaccio, that beat-up fringe of Palermo whose denizens are doubly cursed by Mafia crossfire and urban decay. The atmosphere of violence and crime led the Sicilian-born Puglisi

to take over this godforsaken parish in 1990. Despite his illustrious thirty-year career, he turned down plum assignments in richer neighborhoods. Don Puglisi transformed the church he inherited, the dilapidated San Gaetano, into a literal bully pulpit to fight the Mafia. "He who uses violence isn't a man—he's a beast!" cried the the self-described "ball breaker." The new cleric's sense of humor, affability and fearless stance quickly endeared him to the faithful of Brancaccio. But he made enemies just as fast. The threats began after he denied a Mafia-connected contractor the restoration job on his eighteenth-century baroque church. For this impertinence, the church door was torched and the winning contractor's truck was bombed. To those worried for his life, Puglisi responded, "I have neither wife nor children, and if they kill me, I don't care."

But Don Puglisi did care about the miserable youth he met as a teacher of religion and math. He promoted school activities and social events and, at every turn, vilified the underworld to kids ripe for Mafia exploitation. In 1993, the priest founded the Centro Padre Nostro, a charitable organization for poor families and children. The same year also saw Mafia bombings in Rome and Milan that police connected to Filippo and Giuseppe Graviano, the fraternal bosses of Brancaccio. Puglisi couldn't have picked a fight with more daunting adversaries. The Corleonese honcho Leoluca Bagarella suggested to the brothers that their frocked do-gooder had gone too far. On

September 15, 1993, after celebrating his fifty-sixth birthday with friends, Don Puglisi drove to his apartment around the corner from the church. As he inserted a key into the door, a man stepped up from behind. Don Puglisi smiled and said, "I've been expecting you." The man fired a single bullet into the back of his neck. The priest dropped to the ground, where the blood from his wound welled into a puddle. He died later that night in the hospital.

Father Pino Puglisi's office (left) at the Church of San Gaetano Maria del Divino Amore: Via Brancaccio, 260. The priest was assassinated at the entrance to his apartment: Piazzale Anita Garibaldi, 5.

The news about Don Puglisi, the first clergyman liquidated for preaching against the Mafia, rippled across Italy. The Church, officially opposed to activists in the cloth, was tone-deaf. Pope John Paul II would not break a speaking engagement to attend the funeral and Palermo's archbishop Salvatore Pappalardo skirted mention of the Mafia, saying only that "Puglisi was a priest who disturbed people." The Gravianos were apprehended a few months after Puglisi's death. Five of their lackeys also went to prison for the murder, including triggerman Salvatore Grigoli and his backup man, Gaspare Spatuzza. Both men later claimed a religious conversion. The Church finally recognized Don Puglisi's worth: he was beatified by Pope Benedict XVI in 2013 and his remains were moved to Palermo's cathedral.

SANTA MARIA DEL GESÙ: BROTHER SHOTGUN

High above the cemetery of Santa Maria del Gesù, the resting grounds of many generations of Palermo's noblest citizens, stands the fifteenth-century Franciscan convent of the same name.

Stefano Castronovo, a priest from Agrigento, controlled the order from 1952 until 1980—when Cosa Nostra history was dominated by the neighboring Bontate family. Fra' Giacinto—"Brother Hyacinth," as he was called—with silver pomaded hair and a weakness for Johnny Walker Black Label, was rumored to be mafioso almost from the beginning. The personal confessor of boss Stefano Bontate, he was called "Brother Shotgun" by his detractors. One day in 1964, police inspector Angelo Mangano barged into the convent with a warrant to search for the fugitive Luciano Leggio. The mobster was nowhere to be found, but the rumors about Fra' Giacinto grew more fantastic after that. He was said to lord over a graveyard full of Mafia victims and was a womanizer and a loan shark to boot.

On the morning of September 6, 1980, two stocky men entered the church and waited for Mass to end. The strangers approached the presiding friar and asked to meet Fra' Giacinto. They were directed to a door in the upstairs corridor. When the priest answered their knocking, he was met with a .38-caliber pistol—two shots in the chest and three in the head. He dropped dead instantly and the killers ran off. With the news of the murder came the first glimpse of the mysterious Fra' Giacinto's private life. Police discovered that the avowed Franciscan had claimed a seven-room wing of the convent for his own comfort, including a den furnished with leather chairs, a remote-controlled television and a liquor bar. They found a closet full of tailored suits and English shoes, a collection of cigarette lighters cast in precious metals and, inexplicably, a number of leather riding crops. More ominous was the loaded pistol hidden in a desk drawer and five million newly minted lire. Only after the slaughter of brothers Stefano and Giovanni Bontate, eight months later, could the killing of Fra' Giacinto be seen as the opening salvo of the Second Mafia War.

Franciscan priest Stefano Castronovo claimed a seven-room wing of the convent (above) for his own comfort, including a liquor bar: Convent of Santa Maria del Gesù. Among the tombs in the vast cemetery below is that of anti-Mafia magistrate Paolo Borsellino (see Page 36). A portion of his car-bomb-damaged windshield is incorporated into sculpture. Via Santa Maria del Gesù.

THE CEMETERY OF SANT'ORSOLA

Counterclockwise from top: The tombs of prosecutor Gaetano Costa (see Page 28) and Police Chief Ninni Cassarà (see Page 100) are found in the same same section of the cemetery. Cassarà's nemesis, godfather Michele "the Pope" Greco, lies nearby. Few Sicilians know the location of their most revered Mafia victim, magistrate Giovanni Falcone (see Page 34). He is entombed in his family's gothic mausoleum. Piazza Sant'Orsola.

CIACULLI AND CROCEVERDE

THE FIRST MAFIA WAR

The late 1950s were boom times for the Sicilian Mafia. High-rise apartments shot up in Palermo as fast as corrupt politicos could sign the permits. The new heroin trade promised obscenely high profits to bosses on three continents. Riding high was powerful Mafia Commissioner Salvatore "Little Bird" Greco, an offshoot of the extended Greco clan that overcame terrible family feuds to share the twin suburban thrones of Ciaculli and Croceverde. In 1962, the Grecos were co-investors with the La Barbera brothers of Palermo in Egyptian heroin. When a shipment of dope came up short upon its delivery in New York, all eyes fell on its courier, Calcedonio Di Pisa, another Palermitan on the Commission. Di Pisa was called on the carpet but cleared, only to be gunned down anyway—apparently, the La Barberas didn't buy his plea of innocence. The war was on. Salvatore La Barbera was disappeared, leaving only his smoldering car. His brother Angelo La Barbera struck back by leaving a TNT-charged Alfa Romeo Giulietta outside the Ciaculli residence of Salvatore Greco. The house was ravaged but the boss survived. La Barbera escaped a retaliatory machine gun attack and arranged to kill a Greco family associate, Cesare Manzella, with another exploding Giulietta. Greco predators, in turn, followed La Barbera to Milan and pumped him full of bullets. Miraculously, he lived to fight another day.

A memorial bears the names of the seven the policemen who were pulverized by the car bomb meant for boss Salvatore Greco: Via Gibilrossa, Ciaculli.

A month passed. On June 30, 1963, on the road high atop Ciaculli, an unoccupied Giulietta had appeared. A group of carabinieri and policemen were gathered at the latest of these deadly sports cars, left with its doors wide open. The officers were nervous: already on that morning another Giulietta had exploded in the next town over, killing two. In Ciaculli, military munitions experts arrived to defuse the butane bomb sitting on the backseat. The operation completed, the all's-clear was called, only for an officer to step up and open the trunk, setting off a load of TNT within. Seven were instantly pulverized. The war's heavy body count spurred a police dragnet that pulled in a few thousand mafiosi. The bosses disbanded the Commission. The only complete account of the murky conflict comes from the turncoat Tommaso Buscetta. He claimed that Commission member Michele "the Cobra" Cavataio had started the war to stoke enmity between the Grecos and the La Barberas: the Ciaculli car bomb was never meant for the police but was designed to kill Salvatore Greco. If so, then six years later, Greco got his revenge at the Viale Lazio Massacre.

MICHELE GRECO: THE POPE

Don Michele Greco, the debonair silver fox whose ever-present Bible and prayer cards earned him the nickname "the Pope," was the toast of Palermitan society in the 1970s. He owned a lush expanse of tangerine orchards in Ciaculli with plenty of wild game to excite the sportsmen of the upper classes. Many of the rooms in Greco's lodge had giant ovens and barbecue grills enjoyed by the business leaders, politicians and policemen who were frequent guests of "the Pope." Favorites received their own key to the gate. The Grecos of Ciaculli and the Grecos of Croceverde—related by marriage—were not gentry, they were a criminal dynasty. The parcels of land they held had been wrenched from nobility by intimidating tactics that whittled down the selling price to a nominal fee. Michele Greco's Ciaculli estate, Fondo

Favarella, was the throne of his empire, and supported by roguish relatives like psychopathic killer, Pino "Little Shoe" Greco. Michele Greco's invasive land acquisition, however, was not his attempt to corner the tangerine market. Rather, he sought to control the water below the surface. Although the public owned the water rights, Greco and his fellow mafiosi sold Palermo a third of its supply at a premium. This scheme would have been impossible without the help of able profiteers like Mayor Lima and his public works chief, Vito Ciancimino.

Deep among the citrus trees of Favarella sat a building where the Corleonese syndicate refined heroin, an operation run by Luciano Leggio and Totò Riina. A network of tunnels below the orchards would allow escape during raids. The Corleonesi had pushed Gaetano Badalamenti off the ruling Mafia Commission to make room for Greco, whose legitimizing presence and papal diplomacy swayed decisions in their favor. Dozens of enemies met their end at Favarella following Greco's secret debriefings, including his drug-trade competitor Rosario Riccobono, whose loyalty was suspect. In 1982, as the successful boss slept off a splendid Christmas dinner hosted by Greco and Riina, Little Shoe crept up and strangled him. Several of Riccobono's men were also butchered that evening, then reduced in acid and buried on the grounds. The bloodbath only increased as the power-mad Riina declared war on the state, with the Greco clan often doing the dirty work.

After the police caught up with the fugitive "Pope" Greco, Bible in hand, he assumed the role of a victimized farmer, protesting, "Violence is beneath my dignity. I mind my own business, tending the trees and the land. . . . Even to talk about drugs disgusts me." But aside from a temporary release decreed by Judge Corrado "the Sentence Killer" Carnevale, none of his friends could keep him out of jail. In a cage at the historic Mafia maxi-trial of 1987, charged with seventy-eight murders, Greco delivered a typically cryptic invocation to his prosecutor that was half blessing, half threat: "I wish you peace, Mr. President... because peace is tranquillity of the spirit, the conscience. And for the duty that awaits you, serenity is the foundation on which to judge." On February, 13, 2008, Greco died in prison, at the age of eighty-three, with a Bible by his side.

Fondo Favarella (left), boss Michele Greco's estate and heroin refinery in Ciaculli: Via Conte Federico, 278. He also lived at Via Ciaculli, 461, in next-door Croceverde.

FOUR
BAGHERIA TO SCIARA

BAGHERIA

PROVENZANO'S OFFICE

A secret residence in the corrupted municipality of Bagheria kept Bernardo Provenzano at a comfortable distance from Palermo—and from Totò Riina, his vendetta-bent partner. The once-elegant city of baroque villas had become a Mafia strip mall of profitable business ventures for Provenzano, especially in the areas of public utilities and healthcare, thus earning him the nickname "the Accountant." A former iron mill on a desolate edge of the city became Provenzano's all-purpose office, suitable for meetings and murders alike. Gatherings of the Commission drew Riina and Vito Ciancimino from the west and Catania boss

A former iron mill became godfather Bernardo Provenzano's all-purpose office, suitable for meetings and murders alike: Via Pablo Neruda, 55.

Nitto Santapaola from the east. This old factory, property of a heroin trafficker, featured a drainage pit in the floor that Provenzano repurposed as an acid bath for "tunafish"—casualties of Mafia wars—following interrogation and garroting. One victim was buried in a corner of the plant.

It is ironic that this abattoir would host the first grumbling of dissent among the Corleonese leadership over Riina's bloody war on the state. There was a sense that Riina had gone too far, causing irreparable harm to Cosa Nostra's economic health and political clout. Of the various mafiosi Provenzano assembled at the factory, he took a special liking to Nino Giuffrè, an ex-professor who, in 1980, had joined the Mafia as a driver for Caccamo boss Francesco Intile. After Riina's arrest in 1993, Giuffrè became Provenzano's right-hand "Manuzza," so named for his disfigured hand. Giuffrè shared the capo's desire to steer the Mafia to calmer waters. Rather than turn allies into fearful defectors, as Riina had done, Provenzano and Giuffrè appealed to the moderate mafiosi interested in bringing stealth, efficiency and profitability back to the organization.

TOTÒ CUFFARO AND MICHELE AIELLO: MALPRACTICE

After renouncing the Mafia, Nino Giuffrè described the portfolio of a modernized Mafia in Bagheria: massive shopping malls, futuristic medical centers and other ambitious projects rubber-stamped by elected officials beholden to the bosses for getting the vote. Giuffrè exposed healthcare mogul Michele Aiello, whose state-of-the-art radiography clinic billed the regional government at twenty times the going rate. This facility siphoned both the patients and the funding from the island's decrepit public hospitals. Aiello was frontman for the health-obsessed Bernardo Provenzano—the supremo had laundered close to a billion dollars through him. Greasing the wheels was Aiello's partner Totò Cuffaro, a radiologist and Sicily's governor from 2001 to 2008. Nicknamed "Vasa Vasa"—"Kissy Kissy"—for the pecks he planted on the cheeks of his favor seekers, Cuffaro had the stink of Mafia from the company he kept. The ebullient center-right politician spent much of his time in office fighting charges of criminal association. But his popularity never waned: he won a senate seat in between criminal trials.

Michele Aiello's clinic: Villa Santa Teresa, Highway SS 113. His partner was future Sicilian governor Totò Cuffaro.

Prosecutors learned that Cuffaro had set up "the largest patronage machine ever seen in Sicily, . . . his men placed everywhere," wrote *La Repubblica*. Two of those well-placed men were Aiello's moles who worked inside the very agencies investigating the Mafia. Cuffaro passed official secrets to the bosses targeted in the probes. These crimes eventually sank him. In January 2011, Cuffaro was sentenced to seven years of imprisonment for aiding and abetting the Mafia. A photograph taken at his office the same morning as the verdict shows the grinning governor offering a tray of jumbo cannoli to visitors. The Sicilian sweets were served in celebration, many said, of his having evaded the heavier charge of Mafia collusion. Cuffaro's accomplice Michele Aiello was, however, convicted of collusion, costing him fifteen-and-a-half years.

PORTICELLO

BEPPE MONTANA: LAST PORT OF CALL

Special agent Beppe Montana was shot to death after a boat cruise with friends: Piazza Beppe Montana.

Of the several divisions that make up Italy's state police force known as the Mobile Squad, the Catturandi is charged with tracking down the most dangerous fugitives. Beppe Montana, a young, dedicated cop from Agrigento, led a team of Catturandi through Palermo's dark years of the early 1980s. Like his chief Ninni Cassarà, Montana put himself on the front lines of a raging Mafia war. Both agents of this underfunded unit pursued the mob in their own beat-up cars and scooters like moths drawn to a flame. "We're easy targets," admitted Montana. "And if the mafiosi decide to kill us, they can do it with little difficulty." And yet Montana caused serious harm to the gangs of Palermo with the busts of heroin king Tommaso Spadaro and the killer of Dr. Paolo Giaccone. Montana's tightest focus was on Michele "the Pope" Greco of Ciaculli. The family's gorillas, Pino Greco and Mario Prestifilippo, had already taken out Montana's partner Calogero Zucchetto in 1982. Undeterred, Montana uncovered a Greco arsenal fit for a small army the following year. He later rented a cabin, in 1985, at the edge of Greco territory, where he kept a small boat to conduct coastal reconnaissance of Mafia lairs.

On Thursday, July 25, Beppe Montana's men captured eight of Michele Greco's associates—another victory for the Catturandi. The following Sunday, a jubilant Montana and his fiancée took a few friends out on a boat cruise. While they partied on the water, Greco's gorillas staked out the harbor. After the boat was moored and the revelers stepped on land, Montana was struck and killed by four .38-caliber bullets. While the assassins escaped in a white car, Montana's fiancée ran for help but found the streets were abandoned. One of Montana's friends had noted the make of the white car—a Peugeot—and the first three numbers on the plate. The clue was enough to lead police to the ramshackle house of Salvatore Marino, a young soccer player who had acted as the lookout. Along with the suspect, officers found a bloodied shirt and 34 million lire wrapped in a newspaper bearing the date of the murder. Marino was taken to an interrogation room where he was beaten and tortured throughout the night. He died in transit to the hospital. The police cover story that Marino's death was accidental was blown by the teethmarks in his flesh. This episode was a disgraceful offense that backfired horribly. Marino's mangled body was paraded through Palermo in a white coffin to cries of "Police assassins!" and "*Viva la Mafia!*" But the worst was yet to come to Ninni Cassarà's Mobile Squad in little more than a week.

SANTA FLAVIA

IGNAZIO AND NINO SALVO: TAXING COUSINS

Hotel Zagarella was the place to be seen—and not seen—for A-list mafiosi and politicians of the the Christian Democrat (DC) party. The seaside resort belonged to crooked cousins Ig-

Hotel Zagarella belonged to crooked cousins Ignazio and Nino Salvo, who connected Mafia money to politicians. The resort was recently restored: Via Nazionale, 77.

nazio and Nino Salvo, who made their fortune from ten-percent commissions they earned on the taxes they collected in Sicily. The Salvos were handed that golden concession by Palermo mayor Salvo Lima—a regular at hotel poker games—who, with his criminal deputy, Vito Ciancimino, oversaw the Mafia's "Sack of Palermo." At the peak of their powers, the Salvos picked and financed DC candidates and guided their careers "until the lemon has been fully squeezed." When that happened, the politician would be retired. Though the Zagarella cost $15 million to build, the Salvos chipped in only $600,000, with the balance looted from a government fund for southern development.

The hotel became a flashpoint in the 1993 trial of Giulio Andreotti—"*Il Divo*"—a Roman senator for life, for Mafia collusion. Both an imprisoned Vito Ciancimino and the hotel manager testified that Andreotti was at one of the Salvos' campaign dinners in 1979, but the seven-time prime minister denied having ever known the Salvos. Andreotti maintained the ruse even after a photograph surfaced showing him with Nino Salvo and other mafiosi at a gala featuring heaps of caviar, lobster and suckling pig. State witnesses Tommaso Buscetta and Balduccio Di Maggio's accusation that *Il Divo* was greeted with a kiss by godfather Totò Riina at Ignazio Salvo's home was more shocking. Riina, feeling cut off from Andreotti's protection during the maxi-trials, arranged to have Nino Salvo, the politician's backer, snuffed in 1992.

TERMINI IMERESE

COSIMO CRISTINA: RAILROADED

"There's a body on the rails in the Fossola tunnel!" radioed a lineman to all the trains on the Messina-Palermo line. Each locomotive along the 150-mile route screeched to a halt as railroad employees in Termini Imerese raced into the tunnel. One of the first to reach the bruised body was Luigi Cristina, a man whose twenty-four-year-old son had been missing for two days. He recognized him on the track, dead, with his head bashed in. His son was Cosimo Cristina, the energetic news reporter famous for his crime exposés. Cristina was carrying a suicide letter with a farewell to his best friend and the request that his friend give his fiancée a kiss. There was no mention of Cristina's mother, an unusual omission for someone devoted to his family. Strangely enough, he also carried a soccer pool ticket for a match that had just been played. Cristina's gash was on the wrong side of his head for him to have been hit by the oncoming train. However, investigators waived an autopsy for this "clear case of suicide," over the entreaties of Cristina's family.

Cosimo Cristina's death on May 5, 1960, cut short his already brilliant career in journalism. He wrote for most of Sicily's biggest newspapers before starting his own hard-hitting broadsheet in 1959. Bicycling around Termini in his stylish suit, bow tie and Vandyke beard, he cut the figure of a natty beatnik. But his articles, always bylined "Co. Cri.," were not so tidy. The Mafia was his chosen beat and he raked muck that invited the threats he received. One of Cristina's last pieces, headlined "Agostino Tripi Killed by the Mafia?," convinced police inspector Angelo Mangano of the Mafia vendetta. Mangano had always been troubled by the spots of defecation and swollen bruises on Cristina's body, indicating poisoning and battery. In 1966, Mangano exhumed Cristina's body for an autopsy, but the results were inconclusive. An official plaque placed near the murder site in 2012 unofficially overturns the suicide finding. It reads, "Killed by the Mafia."

The body of journalist Cosimo Cristina was found on the train tracks in the tunnel (above): Viale dei Rei D'Aragona. He is buried in the city cemetery: Via Palermo.

ANTONINO BURRAFATO: BY THE BOOK

Cavallucci's prison complex in Termini Imerese housed a vivid assortment of Mafia characters over the years. Its stone ramparts hosted bandit Salvatore Giuliano's family, corrupted politician Vito Ciancimino and a semi-literate Totò Riina, who passed his grade-school exams while incarcerated. On June 1, 1982, Leoluca Bagarella arrived at Cavallucci fresh from another prison. Like his brother-in-law Riina, the commanding boss was accustomed to a privileged status among inmates. Bagarella's father had just died and he had every expectation of making an unofficial funeral trip to Corleone. But Bagarella hadn't counted on tussling with straight-arrow Deputy Brigadier Antonino Bur-

Cavallucci penitentiary, Via Zara, 28.

rafato, the penitentiary's police chief. This incorruptible officer refused to stretch the rules and denied Bagarella his leave. This infuriated the mafioso. Word of Burrafato's effrontery spread as far as Ucciardone prison in Palermo, where convict Francesco Marino Mannoia heard tales of an altercation in which Bagarella was "banged against a wall." Burrafato expected no repercussions, and the forty-nine-year-old family man continued his routine, including walking the short distance between home and work.

On June 29, a few days after his spat with Bagarella, Burrafato set off for work. Just after 3 p.m. and delayed by his teenage son Totò's excitement over that day's Italy-Argentina World Cup match, four assassins waited for Burrafato in a car. When they spotted him, the driver accelerated while an assassin fired a sawed-off shotgun at him, missing. Another assassin jumped out, fired a .38 five times at his head and chest and left him dead with a disfigured face. A man claiming membership in the leftist Red Brigades took credit for the hit, announcing to a newspaper switchboard operator, "We executed the executioner of Asinara [prison]." The claim was not taken seriously because Burrafato had never worked there. The crime went unsolved for fourteen years until one Palermo boss

Convicted mafioso Leoluca Bagarella sent four assassins to kill prison police chief Antonino Burrafato: Piazza Sant'Antonio.

confessed. He said the death squad, sent by Bagarella, included the heavy hitters Pino Greco and Nino Marchese. The slain officer's son, Totò Burrafato, went on to become the mayor of Termini Imerese. Like his father, he was a stickler for the law and ran his administration free of Mafia intrusion. In 2010, a package was left for him at the door of City Hall, containing a bullet and a letter that read, "You'll meet the same fate as your father."

CACCAMO

THE SWITZERLAND OF COSA NOSTRA

Falcone considered Caccamo "the Switzerland of Cosa Nostra."

In the mid-twentieth century, all of Caccamo's public monies ran first through Don Peppino's fingers. Those wishing to run for office, or buy land or open a shop in the mountain village needed his approval. Of the thirty seats occupied by city council deputies, the one seat that counted was an unelected easy chair reserved for Don Peppino Panzeca. He settled marital disputes and baptized babies on nobody's authority but his own. After Panzeca, a succession of crime bosses in Caccamo led, in the 1990s, to Nino Giuffrè. Under Giuffrè and Bernardo Provenzano's reign, the town became a money laundering haven par excellence. Public contracts were plundered and elections were fixed inside the Mafia's party of choice, the Christian Democrats, and later, Silvio Berlusconi's Forza Italia. When Judge Falcone quipped that Caccamo was "the Switzerland of Cosa Nostra," he wasn't referring to its snowy winter peaks or picturesque castle.

Center-left politician Mico Geraci lived a few blocks up the hill from boss Giuffrè. Geraci began making noise about the fishy situation at City Hall. For his troubles, he received a funereal bouquet of chrysanthemums at his door, then someone set his car on fire. His wife and two children pleaded with him to abandon his plan to run for mayor. But Geraci announced his candidacy in July 1998 and promptly denounced Giuffrè's wife, who had been reinstated as the head of Social Services after being jailed herself for Mafia association. Geraci also decried the local House of Deputies for rejecting a court's order to arrest a Forza Italia member on money laundering charges. On October 8, 1998, as Geraci parked his Vespa in front of the family home, four men in a Fiat Uno pulled up and one aimed a 12-gauge pump shotgun. Buckshot pierced Geraci and left pockmarks on the rolling shutter of the house. Geraci's seventeen-year-old son threw a flower pot at the assassins during the shooting, to no effect. The men surveyed their work then disappeared. Despite several witnesses, including a priest who rushed to Geraci's limp body, no one was ever charged with his murder. But the gunfire had echoed beyond the mountains. Shortly after his funeral, Italy dissolved the city council of Caccamo due to Mafia infiltration.

Clockwise from top left: In Caccamo's city hall, an easy chair was always on reserve for Don Peppino Panzeca: Piazza del Duomo. Under bosses Nino Guiffrè and Bernardo Provenzano's reign, the town became a money laundering haven. Giuffrè lived at Via Liccio, 3. Politician Mico Geraci lived a few blocks up the hill from Giuffrè. As Geraci stepped from his car in front of the family home, he was pierced by buckshot: Piazza Geraci, 41. He is entombed at the cemetery on the hill: Piazza Cappuccini. After Guiffrè repented, his father's grave was bombed by the Mafia.

SCIARA

EMANUELE NOTARBARTOLO: MYSTERY TRAIN

A train bound for Palermo stopped at Sciara long enough to let a distinguished passenger aboard. This notable citizen always carried a loaded gun—bandits had once kidnapped him for ransom and held him in a cave. Feeling secure in his first-class compartment, he unloaded the weapon. But when the train pulled into Palermo, his compartment was empty. Slashed-up, blood-caked seats told a story of murder, while a body lay cold on a railway bridge, the result of the assassins' botched attempt to toss it into the sea. This victim would go down in the annals of Sicily as the first "excellent cadaver," a prominent public servant who got in the way of the Mafia. Marquis Emanuele Notarbartolo was the respected public servant who was stabbed twenty-seven times on February 1, 1893. The crime was shelved as unsolvable in 1895. Notarbartolo's son Leopoldo pulled strings to get the case reopened. The trial was held five years later in Milan. Following the bumbling testimony of the railroad employees who had seen a pair of strangers enter Notarbartolo's compartment, Leopoldo stunned the court—and all of Italy—by accusing Parliament member Raffaele Palizzolo of ordering his father's execution. He then denounced Mafia boss Giuseppe Fontana as the chief assassin.

Marquis Emanuele Notarbartolo boarded the train at Sciara, but his blood-caked compartment arrived in Palermo empty: Via Stazione.

Leopoldo had dug into his father's recent past and come up with a likely motive. Notarbartolo, once Palermo's mayor, was entrusted to repair the Bank of Sicily after stock manipulations by the dynastic Florio family left it floundering. Notarbartolo was opposed by Palizzolo, who was on the bank's board. Palizzolo had prospered by finagling acquisitions of government lands. His extended network of friends—from prosecutors and politicians to mafiosi and brigands—was well known to the police. Notarbartolo had always suspected Palizzolo and his cronies of the kidnapping—the bandits had been arrested for it on the man's property. The trial's exotic tales of Mafia cutthroats and corruption at every level captivated the Italian public. Policemen, politicians and attorneys accused each other of Mafia connivance. The backdrop of political conflict drove various parties, both left and right, to influence the proceedings. The drama intensified when a trembling stationmaster identified one of the strangers on the train as boss Giuseppe Fontana. Both Palizzolo and Fontana were delivered to a courtroom in Bologna for a second trial.

In a hammy performance, Palizzolo portrayed himself as the honest parliamentarian available to constituents. His lawyers described him as "kind, affectionate, a poet in his spare time." Cool-headed Fontana submitted a convincing set of documents from a trip to Tunisia. His alibi stood up after a witness, who saw him near Palermo on the night of the crime, changed his story. After an eleven-month, five hundred-witness trial, Palizzolo and Fontana were each convicted and condemned to thirty years' hard labor. The gallery erupted in cheers. Back home, the Mafia's allies stoked a backlash. Business groups and the press touted the verdict as a reproach of the Sicilian way of life. Palizzolo and Fontana appealed and were retried in Florence, a full decade after the murder, ending in acquittal. Once again, the time-honored grounds of insufficient evidence sheltered the Mafia from the demands of justice.

SALVATORE CARNEVALE: ROYAL PAIN

During World War II, the Mafia's black-market siphon of Sicily's grain crops caused a food shortage among the poor of the island. In 1944, the Communist deputy Fausto Gullo pushed a law through Parliament granting peasants a greater share of the crops. But well into the following decade, rich landholders, like the Princess Notarbartolo of Sciara, refused to give in, relying on hired Mafia guns to keep the hoi polloi at bay. Socialist organizer Salvatore Carnevale staged a successful occupation of her royal estate in 1951. Threatened by gangsters, Carnevale was impeded only by a brief prison sentence. Either to escape another jail term or to evade a boss in Caccamo who had murdered a comrade with a hatchet, Carnevale moved to Tuscany for two years. Reenergized by the advanced gains of the northern activists, he returned to Sciara for another round of land occupations and a suspended jail sentence. In April 1955, Carnevale took a job at a stone quarry on the Notarbartolo estate and rallied the employees to strike against their eleven-hour workday. One mafioso cornered the agitator and said, "If you keep this up, you'll fill a ditch."

Rising before dawn on May 16, Carnevale tried to calm the fears of his mother before beginning his long trek to the quarry in the dark. He reached the dirt path that rose above the town and heard someone call his name. Men with rifles shot him in the hip, the head and the mouth. They smashed his face and left him dead for all to see. When word reached his mother a few hours later, she rushed to the scene but was blocked by carabinieri who told her the body wasn't her son's. Incredulous, she screamed at the brigadier, "They killed him because he defended everyone, my son, my blood! Go search for the killers among the friends and employees of Princess Notarbartolo!" Based on her accusations, the police swiftly arrested four managers of the quarry, three of whom were convicted for the murder and given life sentences. Following their appeals, the Supreme Court overturned the three detainees' verdicts after one witness retracted his testimony. After eight years of confinement, the three mafiosi were again free on the streets of Sciara, rifles hanging conspicuously over their shoulders.

Riflemen killed trade unionist Salvatore Carnevale: Via Cimitero.

FIVE
NORTHERN PALERMO

MARIO FRANCESE: MURDER, INK

A hard-nosed newspaper columnist tailed the Corleonese Mafia's rise to power and reported its every move. His screaming headlines were sacrilege in a land ruled by omertà: "THE INCREDIBLE STORY OF CONTRACTS AND CRIMES AT THE GARCIA DAM: THE MAFIA STRIKES GOLD IN THE MOST BARREN RANCH." The writer launched attack after public attack: "PRIEST: ADVENTURER OR MAFIOSO? This question is asked at every level of public opinion about the peculiar character of Father Agostino Coppola." The priest in question was the frocked mafioso who had presided over the secret wed-

Newspaperman Mario Francese was murdered in the street by Leoluca Bagarella. Francese's son, a budding journalist himself, was among the first to arrive at the scene: Viale Campania at Via Puglia.

ding of Ninetta Bagarella and Totò "The Beast" Riina. Mario Francese scooped the wedding and later secured an exclusive interview with "*La Maestrina*" Bagarella: "ME MAFIOSA? I'M ONLY A WOMAN IN LOVE." Francese hurled his missives from the pages of a Palermo newspaper, the *Giornale di Sicilia*, beginning with the First Mafia War of 1963.

In the 1970s, as a new generation of gangsters and politicians sunk their claws into public works contracts worth billions of lire, Francese named names and printed price tags. Such public exposure could not go unanswered by the Mafia. A plot—the rare one to which Francese was not privy—was hatched by the Mafia Commission of bosses. On the morning of January 26, 1979, Ninetta's brother Leoluca Bagarella emptied a .38 Special into the reporter's head near his home. Shortly after police arrived, Francese's son Giulio, a budding journalist himself, showed up to cover the murder. The unit chief broke the news to him that the bullet-riddled corpse under the sheet was his father. In the 2002 trial of the Francese murder, a defendant recalled the problems his columns caused the Corleonesi. "When news arrived in prison of the death of Francese," he said, "nobody was surprised. It seemed obvious that the murder was ordered and decided by the Commission." Riina, Bagarella and the rest of the Corleonese bosses were found guilty. In 2013, the Garcia Dam was renamed in Francese's honor.

NINNI CASSARÀ: LAST MAN STANDING

In the days immediately following the assassination of Beppe Montana, Police Chief Ninni Cassarà camped out at the station to protect himself. Montana was the second brilliant agent to

Police Chief Ninni Cassarà and his men were met with a rain of two hundred bullets in front of his apartment. Bullet holes are still visible (left). The site is now a gated complex: Viale Croce Rossa, 81.

die since Cassarà took command of Palermo's Mobile Squad in 1981. So many other colleagues had fallen, too—Judge Chinnici and General Dalla Chiesa, Giuliano, Terranova and Basile—tin soldiers toppled in the line of fire. Now, cooped up in his office on the morning of August 6, 1985, Cassarà labored to discover Montana's killers before they killed him. He knew he was the Mafia's prime target. The minister of the interior had arrived from Rome just the day before to break up Palermo's anti-Mafia units—the official response to the murder of Montana as well as the police torture-death of Salvatore Marino. It didn't matter that Cassarà had accomplished so much with so few resources. He and his team had carefully nurtured relationships with key informers to construct an organizational chart of Cosa Nostra. His spy work for Giovanni Falcone and the FBI in New York had helped break the Pizza Connection. Not even a year had passed since Falcone had signed hundreds of arrest warrants that led to the maxi-trials the following year. But that day, Cassarà just wanted to go home. He phoned his wife Laura and told her he'd stop by for lunch.

As always, Laura scrutinized the neighborhood from the balcony as her husband's armored Alfetta pulled up. Cassarà and his two escorts stepped out. In a second, they were met with an explosion of automatic gunfire. A battery of eighteen killers rained some two hundred bullets on their enemies from the building across the street. Pino "Little Shoe" Greco led the assault with his trusted Kalashnikov. His fellow VIPs of the Mafia Commission, Bernardo Brusca and Francesco Madonia, were along for the show. Cassarà, full of bullets, crawled to the apartment staircase but expired from the blood loss. Roberto Antiocha, a young bodyguard who had cut his vacation short to volunteer, was also dead. Laura saw it all. The stage-managed operation could mean only one thing: a mole in Cassarà's office had alerted Greco's squadron to his arrival. Tommaso Buscetta later identified him as Bruno Contrada, the police chief-turned-Secret Services agent who would become associated with the killings of Falcone and Borsellino. The funerals of Cassarà and Antiocha were a disaster. Hundreds of policemen, rancorous as the fall guys in a losing battle, greeted the politicians from Rome with jeers and spit. The minister of the interior ducked out through the side door of the cathedral and made for the airport. A brawl broke out between the cops and the carabinieri. In Palermo's climate of fear and defeat, Falcone and Borsellino were spirited away to a prison island off the Sardinian coast for their own safety.

CLAUDIO DOMINO: MOB JUSTICE

The sensational maxi-trials were front-page news throughout 1986, but the October 9 headline stood out: "The Mafia murders a child to get at his parents." Claudio Domino, the eleven-year-old son of the custodial manager of the court venue, was shot point-blank between the eyes. As public outrage reached fever pitch, many of the mafiosi on trial denied the allegation. Michele "the Pope" Greco and Pippo Calò stood up in their courtroom cages expressing shock and sorrow. Giovanni Bontate, legal advocate for the lot, asked for a moment of silence in memory of little Claudio—which the judge denied—then declared, "We reject the assumption that we could commit such an act of barbarism." In saying "we," Bontate gave away the show. The gangsters' entire defense hinged on their denial that Cosa Nostra existed. It was the first time a mafioso had admitted publicly to membership. But why did the detainees so adamantly decry the murder of a child? Was it simply bad publicity? As turncoat Salvatore Cancemi later explained, the gruesome act was not so much a violation against humanity but a violation of the mob's parallel legal system. To carry out an unauthorized hit on Mafia territory was strictly verboten. Word had gotten out that young Claudio had chanced upon his mother and her secret lover. The lover hastily eliminated the boy and, just as hastily, the Mafia eliminated the lover.

Eleven-year-old Claudio Domino was shot between the eyes for having seen too much: Via Claudio Domino.

ZEN OF INIQUITY

Many of the 16,000 residents of the housing projects known as ZEN—North Expansion Zone—are trapped at the bottom of the Mafia food chain. Built in the early 1970s, the grim

Godfather Salvatore Lo Piccolo made a fortune off of the ZEN housing projects through drug trafficking and extortion: Via P.V. 46.

hive-like tenements, built around courtyards, resemble a monochrome Legoland. TV dishes jut out from the units bearing the names of the politicians who dropped them off in exchange for votes. Officially neglected otherwise—apartments sat vacant awaiting approval into the late 1980s—Cosa Nostra became ZEN's housing authority to families of desperate squatters. It lies in the heart of the San Lorenzo quarter, once the kingdom of godfather Salvatore Lo Piccolo. He made a fortune off the complex through drug trafficking and extorting the tenants for their water and lights. After Lo Piccolo's 2007 arrest, architect Giuseppe Liga took over ZEN's management. His thugs roamed the hallways, collecting payments and thrashing deadbeats. Families who fell behind saw their services cut off for days, or were evicted, their belongings kept as back payment. As late as 2013, Mafia "matchmakers" were known to broker buying and selling of the state-owned housing. In 2008, as police pursued a drug pusher, they discovered a literal underworld below ZEN 2. A remote-controlled door at street level gave them access to a den, thirty-three feet below the surface, used for cutting and packaging drugs. In the room, equipped with air conditioning and a TV, police found a hundred street-packs of cocaine and several thousands of euros. From there, they followed the network of tunnels to a soundproof shooting range of sixty-five square feet, pitted with bullet holes and littered with spent ammo casings from a variety of guns—target practice for the urban hit man.

VILLA PENSABENE: NEW MAFIA DECAPITATED

It had been years since Palermo hosted anything like the Mafia summit of February 7, 2011. The Villa Pensabene, a popular restaurant tucked into a hidden corner of ZEN, was chosen to receive the cream of the bosses arriving from the far-flung corners of the province. As lookouts circled the premises on scooters, fifteen mobsters strolled in, a mixture of old blood and new. A Sicilian antipasto of chickpea fritters and oysters whetted their appetites for the daylong champagne luncheon. The business agenda was full that day: infiltrating jobs at the city's new soccer stadium, vengeance for past offenses and, most important, forming a new Mafia Commission now that godfathers Bernardo Provenzano and Salvatore Lo Piccolo had been arrested. But the diners were unaware they were being monitored in a police barracks through numerous spy cameras. A massive investigation by cooperating authorities had been underway for a year, but this banquet was a revelation. Four bosses in attendance, including Giovanni Bosco, a cousin of Totuccio Inzerillo, had been thought to reside in the US ever since Totò Riina forced them off the island. "Cosa Nostra was attempting to regroup and reconstitute itself," said the Palermo prosecutor after dawn raids in November nailed thirty-six clan members. "With today's operations, we prevented it."

Bosses held a summit at the Villa Pensabene to reconstitute Cosa Nostra after the arrest of its leaders: Via Patti, 99.

SIX
ADDAURA TO MONDELLO

ADDAURA

GIOVANNI FALCONE: NEAR-DEATH EXPERIENCE

In the summer of 1989, Judge Giovanni Falcone was working with two Swiss magistrates on the infiltration of Mafia money into Switzerland. On June 20, he invited his colleagues for supper and a swim at his rented vacation house in Addaura. But the magistrates' schedules were thrown off that evening, so Falcone went to the beach house alone. The next morning, a bodyguard discovered a deadly package deposited on the rocky shore behind the house: fifty-eight sticks of explosives stuffed inside an Adidas gym bag, booby-trapped and detonatable by remote control. An onslaught

Fifty-eight sticks of dynamite were found behind Judge Falcone's vacation house: Lungomare Cristoforo Colombo, 2731.

of anonymous letters aimed at discrediting Falcone had preceded the bombing attempt and made the rounds at the Palace of Justice. The libelous campaign revealed an intimate knowledge of the anti-Mafia pool's investigations. An ally described Falcone's anguish, stating that "he knew in his gut but could not prove that there was a mole with Secret Services connections in the prosecutor's office." Falcone confided to a colleague that he suspected Bruno Contrada, an intelligence agent who would later be convicted for Mafia collusion. A few days later, Falcone said, "They'll try again. The Mafia doesn't forgive and it doesn't forget."

Conflicting testimony stymied inquiries into the assassination attempt. Recent confessions place mafiosi entering the vacation property on land and Secret Services agents arriving by sea. DNA from a sweaty T-shirt found near the bomb implicated Angelo Galatolo in 2011—the Palermo boss had been convicted with other conspirators in the original trial. Another suspect gave a differing account. He testified that mafioso Nino Madonia sat floating in a rubber raft, waiting for the right moment to detonate the bomb. But when he spotted police officers on the shore, he tossed the remote control into the water. The search for the truth continued at a snail's pace. In 2012, the same year an elderly Bruno Contrada was let out of prison on probation, the investigation of the murder attempt ground to a halt. A pair of tweezers used in the DNA testing of a wetsuit and towel found at the scene were deemed "contaminated," rendering the results useless.

JUNIOR'S SAFE HOUSE

In February 2005, while celebrating his birthday in Paris, Massimo Ciancimino received a panicked call from his assistant back in Sicily. He told his boss that carabinieri were at Ciancimino's apartment with a warrant. Captain Antonello Angeli took the phone and assured Ciancimino that the warrant was not for his arrest, but only for a search of his possessions. The devoted son of Don Vito resignedly instructed his assistant to give the agents full access to the property. Among the cache of papers discovered in a false ceiling was, allegedly, the *papello*—godfather Totò Riina's list of demands sent to Don Vito to seal a deal with the Italian government. Four years later, a nervous Angeli told a courtroom that he had discovered the bombshell of a document but was ordered by a superior to leave it in place because a copy was already in possession. According to another officer, Angeli felt bruised by the directive and secretly made photocopies, the likes of which have since disappeared. In September 2010, Ciancimino unexpectedly handed the court forty documents including Don Vito's handwritten notes, Bernardo Provenzano's typed messages and Riina's *papello*. Experts determined the papers to be authentic—except the *papello*.

Among the papers found in Ciancimino Junior's apartment was, allegedly, Totò Riina's list of demands: Lungomare Cristoforo Colombo, 3621.

MONDELLO

SALVO LIMA AND THE SACK OF PALERMO

A building frenzy overtook Palermo in the late 1950s, turning one of Europe's most beautiful cities into a concrete jun-

Said an informer, "[Salvo Lima] was no longer able to protect the interests of the organization at the time of its most important trial." The mayor was being driven in a friend's car when men on motorcycles attacked with guns. Lima bolted from the car but was shot down on the sidewalk: Viale delle Palme, 12.

gle of slapdash tenements. Historic villas and verdant parks were bulldozed as the old center—bombed by the Allies in War War II—was left to rot. New laws granting Sicily an autonomous government were manipulated by a pair of Mafia-connected politicians to drive the land rush. Mayor Salvo Lima and his public works assessor, Vito Ciancimino, doled out billions of lire and thousands of jobs, all on the taxpayer's tab. More than half of the four thousand building permits signed during their partnership were awarded to three old pensioners who had nothing to do with the construction business. The political career of Lima, son of a Palermo mafioso, was sponsored by the bosses of his downtown neighborhood, Salvatore and Angelo La Barbera. Elected to his seat in Parliament's House of Deputies in 1968, Lima solidified his relationship with Giulio Andreotti, a fellow Christian Democrat, who served as the minister of defense. Lima, delivering the DC party votes of Sicily, helped Andreotti win the office of the prime minister in 1972—a formula that would repeat many times over. In 1974, when Lima became Andreotti's undersecretary in the Ministry of the Budget, the cabinet's economist resigned over the appointment "that discredit[ed] the image of the Ministry." Andreotti cut him off mid-speech, later claiming he kept Lima on "to avoid trouble, to make life easier."

Lima was elected to serve as a member of the European Parliament in Strasbourg from 1979 to 1984, while Palermo was in the throes of a Mafia war. The public was demanding action. Cousins Nino and Ignazio Salvo, important funders of Andreotti, were prosecuted in the maxi-trials. The Mafia, with hundreds of its members being prosecuted, turned to Lima and Andreotti for help. Lima attempted to appoint Judge Corrado Carnevale, the infamous "Sentence Killer," but was halted by pressure from the Palace of Justice. Lima's impotence was read by the Mafia as betrayal. Two men on a Honda motorcycle ambushed Lima on March 12, 1992. The politician had just left his home and was being driven in a friend's car to Palermo. The attackers zoomed past, firing guns. The windshield shattered and a front tire was blown out, propelling the car onto the sidewalk. As the bike reversed course, Lima screamed, "*Madonna santa!* They're coming back!" A bullet struck Lima's chest. He threw open the car door but his jacket caught. He ripped it off and bolted down the street, stopping to grab the gate of a house, which was locked. The riders returned, and one of them put a bullet in his head. Lima's assassination was widely read as a warning to politicians who enjoyed Mafia-enabled patronage for decades. "After doing favors for Cosa Nostra in exchange for its votes," said informer Gaspare Mutolo, "[Lima] was no longer able to protect the interests of the organization at the time of its most important trial." More disturbing was an admission from a former colleague, mafioso Tommaso Buscetta: "Salvo Lima was one of the principal political interlocutors of Cosa Nostra, but not the only one."

SEVEN
GIARDINELLO TO SAGANA

GIARDINELLO

THE LO PICCOLOS: DADDY DEAREST

The Catturandi squad, praised for the capture of godfather Bernardo Provenzano in April 2006, was again deployed to bag his presumed successor, Salvatore Lo Piccolo. On the morning of November 5, 2007, forty paramilitary soldiers surrounded a country villa where four Mafia bosses were convened in the garage. An officer shouted the command to surrender. No one emerged from the house, so the agents fired their guns into the air. "We give up!" shouted a young mafioso. When the man appeared, the captors recognized him as Sandro Lo Piccolo, the son of the most-

Soldiers captured most-wanted fugitive Salvatore Lo Piccolo and his son at this country villa: Contrada Partadinello.

wanted fugitive. As the four bosses were disarmed, cuffed and hauled away, Sandro cried to one of them, "I love you, Dad!" The moment was notable not only for its melodrama but for showing the agents exactly which mobster Salvatore Lo Piccolo was. With a helmet of silver hair and a sagging face, the sixty-five-year-old capomafia, sought since 1983, looked nothing like the identikit police had drawn up for him. The bosses wore leather bracelets tooled with religious symbols, like the members of a cult. A cult of Mafia to be sure: the Lo Piccolos had been initiated with the ritual of the burning saint and endorsed an archaic Ten Commandments of the Mafia, found at the scene. On the list of those "who can't be part of Cosa Nostra" were adulterers, relatives of cops and "anyone who behaves badly and doesn't hold to moral values."

Francesco Franzese, the overseer of Lo Piccolo's extortion racket, broke a few of the rules. Captured months earlier, he had tipped off police to the bosses' meeting. The Catturandi seized a duffel bag packed with eight handguns in the villa—one with a silencer attached—and a Holy Grail of hard evidence: Lo Piccolo's business ledger and notebooks full of confidential names and numbers he kept on his person even when sleeping. The capo tried to flush the pages down the toilet during the brief standoff, but they were salvaged and dried, showing police a perfect schematic of the bosses' dominion. Lo Piccolo, a low-key building contractor known as "the Baron," began as a bodyguard for boss Rosario Riccobono and eventually swallowed most of western Palermo. At the time of his arrest, Lo Piccolo was pocketing around $10 million a month from pilfering public contracts, extorting merchants and professionals, illicit construction companies and betting rooms. His right-hand man was his flamboyant son Sandro, aged 32 on his arrest, a suntanned Lothario who counseled lovestruck mafiosi in the art of cunnilingus.

A Polish smuggler busted with a bag of cash put the police onto Paolo Sgroi, head of a Sicilian distributor that stocked the shelves of the Sisa grocery chain. They knew that Lo Piccolo, wiretapped since 2001, laundered his money through this so-called "Supermarket King." They also knew of his desire to expand to America: he had thrown down his welcome mat for the Inzerillo clan keen to come home after their banishment to New York. Despite rumblings of war with rival boss Nino Rotolo, a letter found in the villa contained Provenzano's consent of the Inzerillos' return—if only to keep an eye on them. Newspaper caricatures of the Lo Piccolos as throwbacks to the peaceful Mafia of old were dropped when police announced they had solved the strange disappearance of a merchant. A drawing made by a seven-year-old girl whose father was snatched from the car they were in had baffled investigators since 2000. The sketch depicted the kidnappers as traffic cops. Eight years later, a pair of lowlifes in confinement sang about an abduction involving a fake police stop. They disclosed that Salvatore Lo Piccolo was inside the getaway car, armed with a submachine gun. The victim was interrogated about an old murder, strangled then dissolved in acid. Loverboy Sandro did the strangling himself.

MONTELEPRE

SALVATORE GIULIANO: ROBIN HOODLUM

Bands of outlaws thrived in the mountains of Sicily since at least the fifteenth century. Born of desperation and unbound by laws set up to protect royal landholders, bandits became useful as cutthroats for hire or as partners in black marketing and

Bandit king Salvatore Giuliano often hid on the pyramid-like Monte d'Oro that overlooks his village of Montelepre.

kidnapping. The arrangement ended in 1950 with the death of Salvatore Giuliano, Italy's most famous bandit. Mystery still shrouds the circumstances. Did the murder of the showy young Turiddu, as he was called, come at the hands of the police, Cosa Nostra or even more powerful interests? Whichever the case, travelers often find their way to sleepy Montelepre to visit Giuliano's tomb, one of the few Mafia-related tourist attractions on the island. Giuliano's nascent career as a wartime black marketeer led to the slaying of his first cop, so he took to the foggy mountains around Montelepre with a gang recruited from field workers and army deserters of the impoverished region. Giuliano's long war against the police began when he spied his father being hauled to jail on Christmas Eve of 1943. He instigated a fierce shootout and escaped, leaving an officer dead in the town's central piazza. The legend of Turiddu spread as the result of his daring kidnappings and robberies, one of which included a visit to the boudoir of a rich duchess, where he kissed her hand and politely asked for her jewels. The proceeds of their enterprise were said to enrich the band and ensure its survival in the mountains. Often the sums paid to ransom the kidnapped trickled down to Montelepre's neediest. Reporters came from around the world hoping to get an interview with the Sicilian Robin Hood, who frequently hid on the pyramid-like Monte d'Oro that overlooks the village. He paid visits to his family's home only under the cover of darkness.

Clockwise from top left: Giuliano visited his family only under the cover of darkness. His home is now a museum: Via Castrenze di Bella, 191. When his father was taken to jail, Giuliano instigated a shootout and escaped, leaving a policeman dead: Piazza Ventimiglia. Giuliano's tomb is one of the few Mafia-related tourist attractions on the island. In 2010, his coffin was opened to verify his DNA: Road SP 1.

As a result of the band's crimes, Montelepre turned into a police state. Citizens suspected of aiding the bandit were rounded up and jailed. When the military occupied Giuliano's home in 1949, he fomented an ambush, killing one police officer and wounding two others. Despite his participation in the May Day massacre at Portella della Ginestra (see Page 122) and the cold-blooded murders of numerous policemen, local sentiment still bends in favor of Giuliano. His nephew Giuseppe Sciortino-Giuliano wrote, "People considered Turiddu like a sort of King Solomon.... He reconciled whole families divided by old grudges and he saved many weddings." Conspiratorial whispers followed Giuliano to the grave following his murder. Was he shot down by carabinieri or murdered in his sleep by his closest friend? The most fanciful theory has the bandit king escaping to America. In 2010, the tomb of Giuliano was cracked open by officials, seemingly laying to rest the story that his body was switched at death. After comparing his DNA to that of surviving family members, forensic experts confirmed the authenticity of his remains—with ninety percent certainty. The skeleton is apparently four to eight inches shorter than Turiddu was when alive.

GASPARE PISCIOTTA'S COFFEE BREAK

Gaspare Pisciotta was Giuliano's right-hand man until he betrayed him. His tomb is near that of his former comrade.

Of all the gang members faithful to the bandit Giuliano, it was Gaspare Pisciotta, his former right-hand man, whose life was most in danger following the May Day massacre of peasants. Convicted in the murder trial, Pisciotta was sentenced, along with other perpetrators, to Ucciardone prison, where he shared a protected cell with his father. But Pisciotta was still on trial for the the killing of Giuliano, and he soon confessed to the act. He also accused some important people of other crimes and vowed to expose even more criminals. Pisciotta started writing his memoirs, but someone got to him one morning in February 1954. The cup of coffee he fixed for himself contained enough strychnine to cause a most agonizing death. Was it the sugar, or maybe his vitamin powder? Why hadn't his father died after drinking the same sweetened coffee? Someone had washed all the utensils before the investigators came. Pisciotta's memoirs never materialized. Weeks later, another member of Giuliano's band was similarly poisoned in his Ucciardone cell. This time it was hemlock-laced wine, brought from the outside by "friends."

SAGANA

GIULIANO MEETS THE SEPARATISTS

The rugged mountains surrounding Montelepre gave superior advantages to Salvatore Giuliano over his enemies. He had an eagle's-eye view of the landscape and received intelligence from the local shepherds—an old tradition of banditry. Mount Sagana was the site of the clash between Giuliano's men and the police that ended with the death of band member Rosario Mandela. It was also where Turiddu, at the end of World War II, committed to a radical cause. After the last Fascists had been fought off, the politics of Separatism

At the end of the war, Giuliano was recruited by Separatists during a secret meeting at Sagana bridge. He became a "colonel" for the cause: Highway SS 186.

took hold in Sicily. Military groups hatched a scheme to turn the island into a US territory, and they wanted to train guerrillas in Giuliano's mountains. A meeting with the bandit was set up at Sagana bridge in September 1945. Soon, "Colonel" Giuliano, sympathetic to any underdog's struggle, was born. But this new political alliance was backed by self-interested monarchists and compromised by the involvement of Calogero Vizzini, powerful Mafia boss of Villalba.

EIGHT
PIANA DEGLI ALBANESI TO CAMPOREALE

PIANA DEGLI ALBANESI

MUSSOLINI COMES TO SICILY

The Fascist reign, in the collective memory of Sicilians, was an epoch of repression and violence following Mussolini's 1922 inauguration in Rome. At first, the Mafia bosses enjoyed a boost of prestige as the conservative politicians in their pockets were courted by the early Fascists. But the new prime minister's suspension of electoral democracy in 1925 choked off the bosses' political access. To Mussolini, Sicily was an unruly child in need of the iron hand of Fascist discipline. Reforming Sicily was essential to his establish-

Former City Hall: Piazza Vittorio Emanuele. Mussolini glimpsed the Mafia's power when Mayor Cuccia boasted, "I command this zone!"

ment of an ideal totalitarian state. He glimpsed the island's unique power structure in 1924 during an official state tour of the island. On his visit, Mussolini quickly won over many of the peasants he valorized in grandiose rhetorical speeches. He also took a touristic interest in the colorful Albanians of Piana dei Greci, now called Piana degli Albanesi. Though advised against the visit—the village was thought to be full of Socialist enemies—Mussolini and his entourage, heavy with police escort, wound its way into town.

After the Duce addressed the town's inhabitants with great pageantry, Don Ciccio Cuccia, Piana's mayor, sat proudly next to him in the official limousine. "What's the need for so many cops?" asked Don Ciccio. "Your Excellency is by my side and he has nothing to fear, because I command this zone!" Then, pointing out his own dubious enforcers lurking nearby, the don announced to the villagers, "No one shall touch a hair on Mussolini, my friend and the best man in the world!" Mussolini was stung by the mayor's arrogance. In that instant, he realized that the Mafia's power would have to be smashed if Fascism were to take root. He telegrammed his prefect in Palermo, Cesare Mori, and charged him with organizing a total clampdown of the Mafia, using any means available. "The authority of the state must be absolutely, I repeat, absolutely, reestablished in Sicily," read Mussolini's memo. "If the laws in force are obstacles, this is not a problem. We'll make new laws."

PORTELLA DELLA GINESTRA

THE MAY DAY MASSACRE

Sicilian politics were at a boil in the spring of 1947. With Fascism a fading memory and a population of peasants eager to seize lands promised them, the April 20 elections swung

Sicily far to the left. Feeling confident that a red tide had finally swept in a glorious new era, peasants had something to celebrate that May Day at the workers' festival, held each year in the rocky valley of Portella della Ginestra. Three thousand or more celebrants from the surrounding villages came in old trucks and decorated wagons, on horseback and on foot, with picnic baskets and bottles of wine. By late morning, the grounds were full, children played, red flags soared and songs filled the air. A functionary from the Socialist Party climbed atop a flat rock that served as a stage. "Comrades!" he began. Someone blew off firecrackers. More firecrackers exploded. People dropped, bleeding. Bullets, not fireworks, were coming from nine machine guns on the hill. The crowd dispersed in a panic. Many people were wounded, others were dying or dead—eleven fatalities in all, including three children. The fusillade was heard in Piana dei Greci and the army was summoned from Palermo. Four hundred troops arrived at Portella in the afternoon. The local police, meanwhile, arrested a hundred mafiosi, the likeliest suspects. But each man's alibi was suspiciously, uncannily airtight. Several of them had hosted the chief of police himself at a luncheon that was being served at the time of the slaughter.

Giuliano's men fired nine machine guns from the hill. The stone memorials to the victims have a haunting, runic beauty: Road SP 34.

Only after four local hunters came forth did the details unfold. Confronted by heavily armed bandits that morning, they had been questioned by their leader then shoved into a cave until the shooting was over. The hunters recognized that leader from a mugshot and were astonished to learn he was the famed Salvatore Giuliano. Another four men, out for a frolic in the forest with a prostitute the same day, testified to Turiddu's presence at the scene. The massacre created a national uproar as the Left blamed the Right, along with the Mafia, and the Right blamed the bandits. A great row in Parliament ended in fisticuffs. Witnesses later spoke of a letter Giuliano had received that mandated the attack. After burning it, they reported, the bandit announced to his gang, "The hour of our liberation has come! We're going to attack the Communists, to go fire on them on May 1." Assuring his men that no women or children would be hurt, he reputedly put up a generous sum to hire extra mercenaries and firearms.

After the terrorist act was committed, Giuliano fled. When news of the casualties reached him, he expressed remorse and claimed he'd ordered his men to fire into the air to break up the festival—a sentimental command from a man with so many homicides to his name. In actuality, he had arranged for a second squad to descend from the opposite hill to kidnap and maybe kill Girolamo Li Causi, but the Communist doyen had declined to attend the fair. The greatest hope for the truth about the May Day massacre died in 1950 with the poisoning of Giuliano's closest aide, Gaspare Pisciotta. After having accused those with the most to lose after the elections, Sicily's landholding nobles, Pisciotta was eager to identify other third-party instigators of the tragedy. The case closed a year later. Numerous questions remained but nobody believed the bandits had acted on their own accord.

SAN GIUSEPPE JATO AND SAN CIPIRELLO

GIUSEPPE DI MATTEO: LIFE IN THE DARK

By the end of 1993, a year of heavy Mafia violence, key members were jumping ship. Three detainees confessed their roles in the Falcone assassination—a big break for investigators. The first, Santino Di Matteo, attributed his change of heart to remorse for the victims. He was consigned to protective custody far from Sicily. Based on this new information, the police fanned out with fresh arrest warrants. This made the bosses sweat. Leoluca Bagarella decided that the best way to sew up the mouths of the Judases—and stop future defections—was to make an example of Santino Di Matteo. On November 23, 1993, Giovanni "the Pig" Brusca and five of his men turned up at the stables where Di Matteo's twelve-year-old son took riding lessons. Wearing police uniforms and false mustaches, they told young Giuseppe they were taking him to his father. The boy was thrilled and jumped in their car. But Giuseppe was driven straight to hell, an existence of car trunks, closets and basements. He was often hooded and bound and fed through holes by demons in ski masks. Brusca didn't dare show him his face—Giuseppe would recognize him from the days they played together in the Di Matteos' back yard. As Brusca demanded, his parents said nothing to the authorities about the kidnapping. Ransom notes were sent to Giuseppe's adoring grandfather demanding that Santino Di Matteo take back his testimony. He refused. The old man offered to take his grandson's place instead. Some of the bosses pushed to have the kid killed. Bagarella reprimanded them: "It's wrong to harm even a hair because we're not barbarians."

A farmhouse (top) confiscated from Giovanni Brusca's father Bernardo, the historical godfather of San Giuseppe Jato, is now an agriturismo: Road SP 34. Fourteen-year-old Giuseppe Di Matteo was held captive then killed on the land of a Brusca accomplice. The confiscated property, not accessible to the public, is now used for official ceremonies: Contrada Giambascio near Road SP 3, San Cipirello.

By January 1996, Giuseppe's ordeal had worn on for more than two years. Weak and resigned, he was sealed off in the latest of several hideouts: an underground chamber beneath a house on the land of an accomplice. Brusca felt exasperated. Giuseppe's father still wouldn't recant. Word got out that he often ditched his bodyguards to search for his son in Sicily. And, despite the ski masks, the boy had recognized Brusca and his brother, calling them by name. After Brusca heard a news report that he was given a life sentence based on the testimony of Giuseppe's father, he exploded: "Kill the puppy!" Giuseppe offered no resistance as three of the kidnappers entered his room, roped his neck and yanked him to the floor. Two of them apologized, blaming the boy's stubborn father, then pulled the rope tight. The frail fourteen-year-old quickly suffocated to death. The killers stripped the clothes from his body and dragged him to an adjacent room, where a barrel of hydrochloric acid had been prepared. They carefully submerged the boy and left. In the morning, the men returned. Fishing around in the foul solvent, they found the rope. The only trace of Giuseppe was the darkened tint of the acid.

Brusca ultimately joined the ranks of Santino Di Matteo, "the one who sang," by agreeing to turn state's witness in 1996. Two years later, the ex-mafiosi found themselves facing each other at the Via D'Amelio massacre trial. Di Matteo tore the microphone from its stand and hurled it at the man who had destroyed his son. "I should break your head," he screamed at Brusca. "Animal, you're not worthy to stand in this house!" Turning to the judge, Di Matteo demanded, "President, put us both in that cell over there!"

Counterclockwise from top left: Brusca family tombs in the cemetery of San Giuseppe Jato: Highway SS 624. The location of godfather Bernardo Brusca is apparently undisclosed. This city suffered the greatest losses in the May Day Massacre at Portella della Ginestra. A memorial in the cemetery serves as a mass grave. The names of seven local victims are listed on the wall of City Hall: Via Vittorio Emanuele, 143. At the edge of the building is a fading mural of the atrocity. A memorial to all Mafia victims stands in the adjacent piazza.

CAMPOREALE

THE SINS OF SACCO VANNI

When Vincenzo Ferranti railed against boss Vanni Sacco from the pulpit, the church door was shot up by submachine guns: Church of Sant'Antonio da Padova, Via Atrio Principe, 1.

A devil's triangle of church, state and Mafia once existed in rural Camporeale. The area's capomafia, Vanni Sacco, kept a tight grip on affairs with the help of Palermo's scheming archbishop, Ernesto Eugenio Filippi. A young parish priest named Vincenzo Ferranti railed against Sacco from the pulpit. For this sin, a church door was shot up by submachine guns as he lay in his bed inside. Terrified, Ferranti absconded to Monsignor Filippi's gilded cathedral in Monreale with a young supporter. After Filippi calmed the priest, he arranged a lunch with Sacco and brokered a truce with generous terms for the boss. Before long, a crowd was lured to the piazza of Camporeale by a band playing religious hymns. A convertible automobile rolled up the town's main street carrying a beaming Sacco Vanni. Father Ferranti was seated next to him, chastened and humiliated. In accordance with the agreement, the new church bell was christened with the name of Sacco's daughter, Giovanna.

At the time, activism in the church was being matched by peasant uprisings in the Mafia-controlled fields. In 1948, Camporeale's Socialist mayor, Calogero Cangelosi, led the charge to occupy underdeveloped fields. Laborers showed up en masse, demanding their lawful sixty percent of the harvest. One landholder, Don Serafino, invited Cangelosi to his house in the country for lunch. The mayor accepted over the objections of his fellow party members. When he arrived, he was met by Sacco and his men. They offered Cangelosi a one-way ticket to the United States or Argentina—and even a horse—if he promised to abandon politics altogether. He refused. As his colleagues stormed the house waving guns, the mayor fled. But Sacco wasn't finished with this "hotheaded" Socialist. On the night of April 1, Cangelosi left his office accompanied by four protective friends. As they turned a corner, they were hit with gunfire. Bullets tore through Cangelosi's head and chest. While two of his wounded companions were rushed to the hospital, he was carried to his brother-in-law's house. Cangelosi's wife Francesca was nursing their newborn son when the news arrived. She rushed to the scene but her husband was already dead. The attending carabiniere warned the assembly not to touch the body until an investigator arrived. The corpse lay on the bed for four days, becoming so swollen and black that it no longer looked like Cangelosi. At the funeral, attended by peasants from miles around, Francesca cornered a police marshal and screamed, "They killed my husband and I want justice!" The officer told her to go home, admitting, "We follow orders, but the Mafia gives the orders."

In 1952, the citizens of Camporeale elected the secretary of the local Christian Democrats as mayor. Pasquale Almerico was a one-time schoolteacher who had fought to keep the party free of Mafia infestation. He knew the stakes: he was the young disciple who had fled with Father Ferranti to Monreale. A fresh flow of money into Almerico's party coffers convinced Vanni Sacco

Counterclockwise from top left: City Hall, where two reform-minded men each served a term as mayor during the postwar years: Via Atrio Principe, 10. Socialist Calogero Cangelosi led the charge to occupy underdeveloped fields. Christian Democrat Pasquale Almerico fought to keep his party free of Mafia infestation. Vanni Sacco sent both of them to the cemetery before their time: Road SP 18.

to leave his old Liberal Party behind. When the boss and three hundred of his men made the request to join the DC, Almerico said no. His refusal shocked the region. A directive from party headquarters in Palermo demanded that Almerico "follow the trend of political conditions." He was ostracized by his mates and quickly became isolated. Malicious rumors made the rounds that he was half-mad with syphilis. Failing to receive his party's vote of confidence, the new mayor resigned. But quitting the post would not erase the insolence shown to a "man of honor" like Sacco. Almerico sent frantic pleas to party officials and the police. "His life was in danger," a newspaper reported, "and he mentioned the names of some of the people who had forewarned him of the Mafia's vendetta." Almerico ate his last dinner alone at the town social club on March 25, 1957. Feeling fearful, he asked his brother to accompany him home. As they stepped into the night air, a power outage plunged the streets into darkness. Five men with submachine guns opened fire and Almerico dropped. At the morgue, 111 bullets fell from his perforated body. Vanni Sacco was twice arrested for Almerico's murder and twice released for insufficient evidence. The boss grew to influence the DC well into the 1970s.

NINE
PARTINICO TO MONREALE

PARTINICO AND BORGETTO

THE VITALES: FAMILY FEUD

It was a police riot in reverse. As news cameras rolled, a dozen or more people broke through a security cordon and began punching and kicking agents of the Flying Squad. The wife and children of Vito Vitale, who was arrested on April 24, 1998, were among the relatives assaulting officers charged with transporting the Partinico boss to prison. "Fardazza," as he was called, was the third Vitale brother to be sentenced to prison for Mafia crimes, following Leonardo and Michele. So high had Fardazza risen in the organization that, after the capture of Totò Riina, some investigators considered him the new leader of the Corleone mob. His close alliance with the Corleonesi was based on the fact that he could "shoot like a god," according to an informer. The Vitales' takeover of the Partinico underworld, in the early 1990s, came as the result of a dispute over hierarchy. Riina's right-hand man, Bernardo Provenzano, supported the old Partinico boss Nenè

The home of Partinico boss Vito "Fardazza" Vitale (left) was turned over to an anti-Mafia group in 2012: Via Foscolo, 123. The crimes of the Vitale family were regularly documented on broadcasts emanating from the studios of Telejato, a fiercely anti-Mafia TV station: Via Francesco Crispi, 33. Vitale's teenage son attempted to strangle news anchor Pino Maniaci with a necktie.

Geraci, a ranking member of the Mafia Commission whose yes votes on Riina's assassinations landed him twelve life sentences. But younger bosses such as the Vitales, Giovanni Brusca and Matteo Messina Denaro feared Provenzano's risky antics—the fugitive godfather took to being chauffeured around Palermo dressed as a priest.

Riina capitalized on the anti-Provenzano sentiment and deposed Nenè Geraci, installing the Vitales as the new leaders of Partinico. Geraci's namesake younger cousin was removed as well, with five bullets, as he took his coffee. But after the 1998 arrest that completed the incarceration of the three Vitale brothers, the rule went to their sister Giuseppa, popularly known as Giusy—pronounced "juicy." As ruthless as her brothers were, Giusy carried on the family business and even decreed murders until she was thwarted by the law and undone by maternal inclinations. Not only was she the first woman to be convicted and sentenced for Mafia association, she was also the first female turncoat. In February 2005, exposing the family secrets, she blew the whistle on several double-dealing politicians and businessmen. "I did it for the sake of my children," she said. "If I'm in prison, I'll lose them." During one court hearing, her brother Leonardo fumed over his sister: "We disown her whether she's alive or dead. And we hope it'll be the latter—as soon as possible."

GIULIANO'S RED SCARE

When Salvatore Giuliano and his men became the chief suspects in the May Day massacre at Portella della Ginestra, the bandit fired off letters to newspapers and politicians proclaiming his innocence. He accused the carabiniere of extracting tortured confessions that placed the blame on him. Playing up his heroic Robin Hood image, he tried to reason with the readers of a Communist newspaper, asking how he, "the defender of the poor and the enemy of the rich," could possibly commit such atrocities. Giuliano soon undermined his protests by mounting a twenty-four hour terror campaign against leftists across Palermo province. On the night of June 22, 1947, an orchestra playing for an audience in the piazza of Partinico was suddenly drowned out by explosions and gunfire. As the crowd dispersed, two officers of the carabiniere rushed around the corner toward the source of the racket. They found a blazing sidewalk in front of the local headquarters of the Communist party. Cabinetmaker and party member Giuseppe Casarrubea was lying dead in a pool of blood. Five others were wounded, one man still clutching a handgun he never got the chance to fire. Three bombs had blown open the building but two other bombs remained unexploded. Police collected forty-one cases of 9mm machine gun cartridges and the remnants of Molotov cocktails and hand grenades. Thousands of handprinted leaflets announcing a battle against Bolshevism

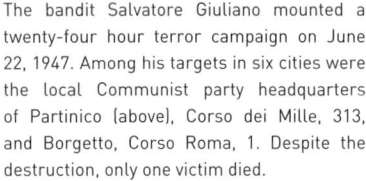

The bandit Salvatore Giuliano mounted a twenty-four hour terror campaign on June 22, 1947. Among his targets in six cities were the local Communist party headquarters of Partinico (above), Corso dei Mille, 313, and Borgetto, Corso Roma, 1. Despite the destruction, only one victim died.

littered the surrounding alleys: "The decisive hour has already struck! He who does not want to be easy prey to that baying pack of reds . . . must today decide. Those people who want at every cost to throw us into the lap of that terrible Russia . . . must be fought without ceasing." The manifesto was signed by Giuliano.

Less than two hours after the Partinico attack, two men disguised as carabinieri opened fire on Communist headquarters in the adjacent town of Borgetto. Soldiers stationed in barracks nearby believed they were under attack while civilians thought it was the real soldiers firing. Similar strikes were made on Communist and Socialist offices in San Giuseppe Jato, Carini, Monreale and Cinisi, all before the sun rose. More of Giuliano's leaflets were left fluttering in the streets. Whatever the intrigue at play in his coordinated actions, it was clear to everyone that he was out of control. His band's incursions of June 22 cost only one life, but nine other assassinations of carabinieri already had stained his record and the outrage from the Portella massacre was still fresh. For all the bombast of his attacks and the all bluster of his manifestos, Giuliano quit his anti-red crusade. As Sicily's most wanted and most reviled man, his goal became survival.

MONREALE

THE DOUBLE DEATH OF GIULIANO

Villa Carolina, on the outskirts of Monreale, is a significant, if weathered, landmark in Salvatore Giuliano's story. He and his followers used it as as hideout and a place to stow their kidnapped victims. The villa had fallen into the hands of a devious shepherd named Netto Minasola, who did business with both the bandits and the local Mafia. In 1950, three years after the May Day massacre, the coalition of law enforcers on the case were frustrated by their inability to smoke their main suspect, Giuliano, out of hiding. They threatened Minasola into cooperating. The miscreant recruited his Mafia friends and, together, they led the carabiniere to two members of Giuliano's gang in Sagana. After an exchange of gunfire, soldiers shot one bandit dead but the other got away. Minasola knew the escapee would make his way to the Villa Carolina. When he did, Minasola turned him over to the carabinieri waiting for the bandit in a dark room. Meanwhile, Giuliano was hidden in a house in Castelvetrano, where he would be killed in short order (see Page 203).

Villa Carolina was a favorite hideout of Giuliano and his bandits. Some believe he was murdered here: Highway SS 186 at Road SP 69.

Giuliano's surviving family clings to an alternate version of his death. As the story goes, Turiddu hid in the house in Castelvetrano. When he got word that his lieutenant Gaspare Pisciotta betrayed him, the outlaw rushed to the Villa Carolina to confront him. "How can you have doubts about me?" protested Pisciotta, who laid out a meal for his comrade. The suspicious Turiddu sat down to eat without removing his gun. Suddenly drowsy, he moved to the bedroom and passed out—the effect of sleeping powder Pisciotta had sprinkled into his wine. The police had supplied the drug and released a former band member from jail to help. The traitors bound the unconscious Turiddu's hands and feet to the bed. Pisciotta then left the villa to fetch the pair of mafiosi involved in the plot. But he wasn't aware that his fellow bandit had already negotiated a separate deal with the police. Swayed by the promise of reward money and freedom, the accomplice aimed his gun at his former chief, closed his eyes and fired three times. When Pisciotta and the mafiosi returned to find Giuliano murdered, they panicked at the implications. But soon, the officers who had set up the scheme arrived and calmed the conspirators. The captain then devised a plan to deliver the body to a house in Castelvetrano Giuliano was known to frequent. The colonel grabbed the bandit's diary containing "all the truth" about the May Day massacre. As the body was dressed for transport, the officers divided the cash they swiped from the dead man's pocket—money collected for his escape to America.

EMANUELE BASILE: FEAST OF DEATH

Emanuele Basile, captain of the carabiniere unit in the cramped hilltop town of Monreale, had been in the Mafia's gunsights since he revived the drug cases of his murdered predecessor,

Police Chief Boris Giuliano. Basile's home was under lockdown and the threats he received made chilling references to his four-year-old daughter Barbara. Basile and his wife took Barbara out of nursery school and the family mostly stayed home during the spring of 1980. The previous summer, following Boris Giuliano's murder, the carabiniere arrested his likely assassin, Leoluca Bagarella. Captain Basile indicted him for narcotics trafficking and locked up his crew. He then followed the trail of evidence to Bologna, where relatives of Luciano Leggio and Totò Riina supplied heroin to the northern city's large junkie population. Basile's friend and colleague Paolo Borsellino accompanied him to Bologna to interrogate the traffickers. A seizure of bank records from the home of Riina's uncle gave Basile the proof he needed to identify the sundry operatives of the vast drug ring.

A pair of commemorative plaques marks the spot where Captain Emanuele Basile was assassinated: Piazza Calcedonio Inghilleri.

A few weeks later, on May 4, 1980, Basile treated his family to a rare outing for Monreale's annual Feast of the Holy Cross. Afterwards, they walked homeward, little Barbara asleep in her father's arms. Three men advanced on Basile from behind and fired six shots. Father and daughter dropped to the ground as wife Silvana threw herself over them. Silvana looked up and met the eyes of the gunmen before they took off. One took a shot at her from a distance but missed. She turned her attention to little Barbara, removing the motionless girl from her father's embrace. As she wiped the blood from her child, Silvana realized it had come from Basile's fatal wounds, not Barbara, who was now awake and completely unharmed. Basile's killers were captured before sunrise. Borsellino noted that the death squad of Giuseppe Madonia, Armando Bonanno and Vincenzo Puccio represented three Palermo families that Captain Basile had investigated. With witnesses and evidence—mud on the men's clothing came from the crime scene—the murder trial should have been open-and-shut. But a series of hearings was complicated by obstructionist judges, intimidated juries and the suspects' banishment from Palermo that eased their escape. Puccio and Madonia were eventually caught, convicted and, after a few appeals, all three slayers received life sentences.

TEN
CASTELLAMMARE DEL GOLFO TO CAPACI

CASTELLAMMARE DEL GOLFO

JOE BANANAS

The roots of the American Mafia sprang from Castellammare del Golfo, an ancient port built in the shadow of the Norman castle that gave the city its name. Salvatore Maranzano was already a powerful New York mobster when fellow Castellammare hoodlum Giuseppe "Joe" Bonanno, fleeing Fascist Sicily, joined his gang as an enforcer. Both men had been raised in old Sicilian "tradition," to use Bonanno's word, bound by tribal suspicion of outsiders and duty to defend family honor to the death. The principles were useful during Prohibition—the gang's Castellammarese allies controlled bootlegging from Manhattan to Detroit. But greed would trump blood when Maranzano tried to muscle in on the business of rival boss Joseph Masseria, igniting the bloody "Castellammarese War." It came to an end in 1931 when Maranzano convinced Lucky Luciano to betray Masseria, the Sicilian hit man's boss. Celebrated in the annals of gangland

Locally refined heroin departed from the Castellammarese bay on ships bound for America, packed in canned foods and oranges: Via Don Leonardo Zangara.

history, Luciano, dining with Masseria in a Coney Island restaurant, ducked into the restroom just before his boss was shot to death. Luciano double-crossed Maranzano later that year by having him murdered as well.

Luciano carried on with restructuring the Mafia into the Commission that Maranzano had introduced. He divided the region into territories to establish the Five Families of New York in a power-sharing arrangement that would continue into the twenty-first century. With Maranzano gone, Bonanno—Joe Bananas in America—inherited the prized territory of Brooklyn. He ruled the crime family for decades in Old World "tradition" that included a Sicilian-only language rule.

In October 1957, Luciano and Bonanno reconnected with the Sicilian Cosa Nostra at the Palermo summit convened to establish a narcotics accord. Castellammare del Golfo was strategically close to the secret heroin refineries that soon popped up. The precious contraband departed from the bay on ships bound for America packed in canned foods, oranges and even marble from the local quarries. Bonanno, who had received a hero's welcome in Palermo during the summit, was arrested in November with sixty other American mobsters at the New York estate of Joseph "Joe the Barber" Barbara—another mafioso from Castellammare. The lineage of the Five Families was still evident in 2011 with the killing of Salvatore Montagna, thirty-six-year-old captain of the modern Bonanno family. Deported from the US to Canada, the "Bambino Boss" was a Montreal-born loan shark who had been raised in Castellammare del Golfo.

ALCAMO MARINA

THE CARABINIERE MASSACRE OF 1976

A politician and his police escort were driving along the shoreline road of Alcamo Marina on the frigid morning of January 26, 1976, when something caught the eye of a bodyguard: the door of the local carabiniere barracks was wide open. Stopping to investigate, the policemen stepped inside and found two dead soldiers, full of bullets, sprawled on the floor in a puddle of their own blood. The victims, Lance Corporal Salvatore Falcetta and officer Carmine Apuzzo, apparently

The names of the two murdered carabiniere soldiers are remembered on this obelisk. The crime took place in the former barracks (not pictured), next door to the east : Highway SS 187 near Contrada Alcamo Marina.

had been attacked in their sleep and robbed of their service arms and uniforms. That day, a newspaper office was contacted by an anonymous caller who said, "The people and the workers bring justice to all the slaves and ranking carabinieri who defend the bourgeois state." Colonel Giuseppe Russo of Ficuzza organized a manhunt to find the extreme-left terrorists. Three weeks later, one Giuseppe Vesco, driving a Fiat 127, was stopped at a police roadblock and found to be packing a revolver. A search of his car produced a conclusive piece of evidence: the carabiniere-issue Beretta 9mm Parabellum that proved to be the weapon used to kill the soldiers. Vesco had the record of an active Anarchist—a mishap with an explosive device had required the amputation of his hand. After a night of grilling, he named four accomplices: Giovanni Mandalà, in whose barn he claimed to have found the weapon, Giuseppe Gulotta, Gaetano Santangelo and Vincenzo Ferrandelli. But an unusual detail was ignored as they awaited trial: with the exception of Mandalà, the suspects of the cold-blooded act were all between the ages of sixteen and nineteen.

Vesco took back his words a few months later, claiming his confession had been extracted by torture. Yet days before his hearing, the one-handed youth managed to commit suicide, according to the prison authorities. Mandalà and Gulotta were given life sentences and Santangelo and Ferrandelli, minors at the time, got twenty years apiece. The allegations of torture put retrials into motion and, in between appeals, Santangelo and Ferrandelli escaped to Brazil. After serving several years of confinement, Mandalà died. That left only Giuseppe Gulotta doing time for the massacre, despite his own claims of a confession borne from torture. At the eventual retrial in 2008, Renato Olino, a retired brigadier and one of the original investigators, showed up unexpectedly to corroborate the prisoners' claims. Giuseppe

Vesco, Olino testified, had been induced to confess by means of the *cassetta*, a wooden crate on which he was bound. As one officer pinched his nose shut, another poured a bucket of saltwater into a funnel stuck in his mouth. Electrical shocks from live telephone wires were administered to Vesco. Olino added that a gun had been pointed at the boys' heads in mock execution. The barbarity, he said, was approved by Colonel Russo, who was later killed by the Mafia. In 2012, all of the accused, alive or dead, were exonerated. Hypotheses about the 1976 massacre vary. One scenario has the soldiers stumbling upon a truck delivering weapons to a secret NATO Gladio base. But the crime was more likely just part of the larger political atrocities committed, during the late twentieth century, in the name of Mafia supremacy.

TRAPPETO

DANILO DOLCI: BIGGER THAN THE MAFIA

When Danilo Dolci stepped off the train in 1952, he was ready, as a peasant who knew him wrote, "to share the life of the poor." As a teen, he had seen things that disturbed him while visiting his father, who served as Trappeto's wartime stationmaster.

When Danilo Dolci arrived in 1952, Trappeto resembled a famine-ridden village of Africa.

After the war, he remained haunted by images of emaciated children living on beans and bugs, fathers forced into banditry and fat government officials. Violently abused by his father, the wide-eyed poet had grown into an activist who cared for orphans in the north. His credo was, "Participate in order to understand." In the 1950s, Trappeto was a fishing village that resembled a famine-ridden village of Africa. For years, Mafia-backed fishing pirates bombed the Castellammare Bay at night and scooped up the tons of sardine fry that surfaced, leaving little for the local fishermen to scrounge. The state did nothing to stop the ruinous practice. With farms and irrigation under Mafia control, grain was inaccessible to the peasants. Dolci wrote letters to influential people in Rome. He ventured to distant towns to procure medicine for others on credit. He announced a hunger strike, declaring, "From today on, I shall not eat another mouthful of food until the thirty million lire required to employ the neediest and help the most urgent cases has arrived."

Within a week of fasting, Dolci suffered a stroke. But word had already reached Palermo and money arrived just in time. Suddenly, he could break ground on his greatest ambition to date, a house for the most destitute of Trappeto, naming it the Borgo di Dio—the Hamlet of God. Dolci was able to finance construction of the Borgo on credit, his only collateral being promises, good will and a glowing reputation. Dozens of unemployed men hauled materials up the hill overlooking the sea, confident of a distant payday. When Dolci's promissory note to a furniture shop went unpaid, he surrendered his scooter to the threatening dealer. The Borgo opened its doors in 1953. The first occupants were a couple whose baby had died of starvation a few days before. They were joined by a woman with five children whose husband had been beaten to death by bandits. The rare sight of bread on the table drove the little ones to hide loaves under their pillows lest they vanish like a dream. Though he was a published poet in Italy, Dolci's sociological books traveled as far as the US. He recorded many people on tape, from the poorest peasant to Cardinal Ernesto Ruffini of Palermo, who later branded Dolci an enemy of Sicily. He even published an interview with the ill-famed capomafia Giuseppe Genco Russo, in a chapter titled "The Parasite Cultures." Unlike so many other anti-Mafia activists, the peaceful rabble-rouser outlived his Mafia contemporaries. Dolci died in 1997 at the age of seventy-four.

Counterclockwise from top left: Dolci opened the Borgo di Dio—the Hamlet of God—to house the most destitute of Trappeto The structure is still visible through overgrown brush: Via Borgo di Dio. His remains stayed in the village cemetery: Highway SS 187 Ovest.

CINISI

DON TANO AND THE PIZZA CONNECTION

In the First Mafia War of 1963, a car bomb splattered the guts of Cesare Manzella across the lemon trees of his Cinisi estate. Gaetano Badalamenti, the godfather's second-in-command, took over the lobbying effort, with bribe money, to ensure Palermo's new airport be built at the edge of the seaside town. What en-

Drug trafficker and Cinisi godfather Gaetano Badalamenti lived at Corso Umberto I, 183.

terprising mafioso wouldn't set up lucrative construction contracts or receive airborne shipments of contraband in his own backyard? The gusty airstrips built at the foot of a mountain made mockery of safety standards. The Commission of bosses, disbanded since the Mafia War of 1963, was resuscitated in the early 1970s under the direction of Gaetano Badalamenti, Stefano Bontate and Luciano Leggio. When "Don Tano" Badalamenti was jailed briefly, Leggio and his Corleonesi elbowed him off the Commission to cement their power. But Don Tano was going international, soon to pop up in the US, Brazil, Bolivia and Spain. One of history's most accomplished drug traffickers, he oversaw the refinement of Middle Eastern heroin in Sicily for distribution in sham pizzerias along the US eastern seaboard—the famous Pizza Connection, worth $1.6 billion during its operation.

In 1984, the FBI and cooperating agencies busted Badalamenti in Madrid and placed him in a New York courtroom to stand trial with dozens of global accomplices. Much of the damning testimony came from Tommaso Buscetta, the envoy Badalamenti had sent to Canada to set up a heroin depot. For his role as the ringleader of the Pizza Connection, Don Tano, exceedingly polite but never self-incriminating, received forty-five years. In 1993, Buscetta again mentioned Badalamenti's name to prosecutors, claiming the boss was a participant in the 1979 murder of the blackmailing reporter Mino Pecorelli in Rome.

Badalamenti, said Buscetta, considered the killing a personal favor to then-acting Prime Minister Andreotti. If nothing of legal consequence came of the accusation, the scandal illuminated ties between the Mafia and the Christian Democrat party. Forty-five years was the lesser of Badalamenti's sentences. In 2002, he was condemned to life for mandating the 1978 murder of Cinisi activist Giuseppe Impastato. After Don Tano's death, in 2004, his body stayed in America. He is represented in the family mausoleum by a small framed photograph.

THE HUNDRED STEPS OF PEPPINO

Giuseppe "Peppino" Impastato should have grown up to become a "man of honor." He was raised in Cinisi, the small town that was, in the 1950s, buzzing with Mafia activity. His father was a low-level mafioso and his aunt was married to the old godfather, Cesare Manzella. Peppino lived a hundred paces from the new godfather, Don Tano Badalamenti, who took over after Manzella was blown up. The fifteen-year-old boy was horrified and disgusted by his uncle's murder. He wanted no part of the Mafia. The boy was already developing a political consciousness—he attended Communist meetings with another uncle and became hooked. Soon, Peppino and his friends launched a Socialist newspaper that took on the full range of Sicilian issues, from sexism to the Church. But especially, they attacked Cosa Nostra and its politicians. To a town where elected officials and cops chatted amiably with mafiosi in public, this was blasphemy. When the paper's first issue came out, the young activists were made to answer to the police. Another, headlined, "The Mafia: A Mountain of Shit," occasioned a visit to the Impastato house by an angry old don. Peppino's father Luigi was humiliated and he kicked his eighteen-year-old son out of the house. Peppino further divided his family—and most of Cinisi—by founding the Che Guevara Club and preaching Maoism in the streets with his longhaired comrades.

1976 was a watershed year for Peppino. He ran in regional elections, losing with a respectable four percent of the vote. More significantly, this revolutionary with the soul of a poet started a film club and a radio station from which he broadcast creatively incendiary material. Suddenly, Don Tano himself was issuing threats to Luigi, who begged for his son's life. Not long after, Luigi was run over and killed by a driver who said it was an accident. But relatives remembered his words: "I've told them, 'They'll have to kill me first before they kill Peppino.'" By 1978, Peppino was carrying the burden of national politics on his shoulders. Preoccupied with the "historic compromise" between the Italian Communist Party and the Mafia-tainted Christian Democrats, the already gaunt man was weak and barely eating. But his attacks on political enemies only intensified. He curated a photo exhibit on Cinisi's main drag that exposed the runaway development unleashed by the Mafia under City Hall's approval. And he launched another electoral run, peppering his campaign speeches with the names of wrongdoers.

Shortly after midnight on May 9, 1978, the operator of a train felt a jolt on the track near Cinisi and pulled to a stop. He discovered torn rails and the dismembered parts of a human body. When the police arrived, they found flesh, bones and clothing spread across a thousand-foot radius. A piece of a human face, eyeglasses, a pair of clogs and a car parked next to a shack were all recognized as belonging to Peppino. A set of bloodstains inside the shack went ignored. On the same day, another calamity occurred: the Christian Democrat leader Aldo Moro was assassinated by his Red Brigade kidnappers in Rome. Not only did this shock bury the news of Peppino's death, it also gave Sicilian authorities a handy explanation: Impastato, the left-wing "terrorist," had blown himself up to derail a train. The rushed investigation smelled of a coverup. Whatever bits of Peppino hadn't been removed by neighbors or crows were collected by friends for forensic study. The blood inside the shack proved to be of the same rare type as his. It took the activist's mother, brother and friends years of lobbying to bring to light what they knew all along: that Giuseppe Impastato had been abducted and brought in his car to the shack, where he was tortured and killed. His captors had then lashed sticks of dynamite to his body before placing him on the tracks and blowing him up, condemning the Mafia fighter to the same fate as his uncle, the old godfather of Cinisi.

Clockwise from left: Giuseppe Impastato's house is now an anti-Mafia museum, Corso Umberto I, 220. The Mafia fighter was abducted then tortured and killed in a shack behind Via Paolo Borsellino, 37. He is interred in the family mausoleum: Via Palermo near Highway SS 113.

TERRASINI

RADIO AUT: MAFIA IN THE MIX

Impastato started Radio Aut to battle the Mafia: Corso Vittorio Emanuele, 108.

Giuseppe Impastato used every available medium to battle the Mafia. In 1976, he founded a small FM radio station and called it Radio Aut. His signature show, *Onda Pazza*—"Crazy Wave"—was a series of satirical dramas about life in "Mafiapoli," a substitute for Cinisi. Music and sound effects wryly underscored the dialogue of Peppino and friends. Local politicians were lampooned mercilessly to the porcine snorts of Pink Floyd's "Pigs." An obvious caricature of Don Tano Badalamenti depicted the capo praying for a Christian Democrat win, mixed with the ricochets of bullets from an old western. Young people brought portable radios to bars and listened in groups. The show was a hit. Three days after one particularly caustic broadcast, Impastato was blown up. But the scandalous tapes he left behind took on a new life one year later: *Onda Pazza* was played from loudspeakers that lined Cinisi's main street as two thousand activists marched to remember his death. In 2000, a film dramatization of Impastato's life, *I Cento Passi*—"The Hundred Steps"—was a smash success. His mother Felicia was embraced by activists of the growing anti-Mafia movement. Impastato's house became a center of anti-Mafia organizing. In 2010, Radio 100 Passi began broadcasting from the house, in the defiant spirit of Radio Aut.

VILLAGRAZIA DI CARINI

ANTONINO AGOSTINO: EMPTY CLOSET

It had been a hasty but happy wedding. The twenty-eight-year-old policeman Antonino Agostino and his nineteen-year-old bride Ida—five months pregnant—were back home in Palermo following their honeymoon in Greece. Although his family knew he was gravely preoccupied with a confidential matter at work, Antonino did his best to hide it. On August 5, 1989, all the relatives were gathered in a rented villa on the sea for another celebration: the birthday of Ida's sister. But an approaching roar of motorcycles disrupted the party. A group of gunmen burst in. Antonino called out, telling Ida to run. She screamed at one of the intruders, "I know you!" Bullets starting flying. By the time the shooters retreated, three were dead: Antonino, Ida and their unborn baby girl. Amid the terror and confusion, Antonino's father Vincenzo searched his dead son's pockets and found a card on which he had written, "If anything happens to me go and look in my bedroom closet." But

The killers of policeman Antonino Agostino and his pregnant wife are still unknown: Lungomare Cristoforo Colombo, (formerly) 699.

while Vincenzo kept vigil over the bodies at the mortuary, a pair of police officials paid a visit to the newlyweds' home first. Ida's sister was there and let them in. After their search, the agents left with an envelope they'd found in Agostino's closet.

For months after the homicides, investigators chased a false lead: an imagined crime of passion by Agostino's old flame, the daughter of a Mafia boss. As the decades wore on, the unsolved crime was found to be hopelessly entwined with the darkest mysteries of the state, the Mafia and the assassinations of Falcone and Borsellino. Seven months after Agostino's death, an ex-cop working for the Secret Services, Emanuele Piazza, vanished without a trace. According to several insiders, Agostino and Piazza had together investigated the attempt on Falcone's life at Addaura, though officials denied it. Two others connected to the Addaura incident were also killed. An authoritative journalist hypothesized that Agostino and Piazza had been the two men seen in a rubber raft in the waters behind the judge's vacation home. The scenario had the two agents in scuba gear swimming to shore, on behalf of the Secret Services, to dismantle the bomb planted by the Mafia. But Vincenzo Agostino would not have the theory, explaining that his son "has never gone skin diving. He suffered from apnea." The elderly man with long white locks and a bushy white beard vowed to cut his hair only after Antonino's killers were identified.

CAPACI

FALCONE'S DEATH: OF MEN AND MONSTERS

Exactly halfway on the highway between the airport and Palermo is Capaci, a drab town tumbling from the rocky foothills to the sea. Beneath a section of the highway was a metal culvert that drained the area of its copious rainwater. In late April of 1992, a crew of five men disguised as maintenance workers labored in the dark of night. Using a skateboard, they slid thirteen barrels packed with TNT and gelignite into the culvert. The crew hid the explosives behind a mattress and dragged an abandoned refrigerator to a spot eighty feet away as a reference for three men on the hill. One of them, Giovanni "the Pig" Brusca, sat with a radio-frequency device poised to detonate the nearly half-ton bomb at precisely the second Judge Giovanni Falcone's motorcade passed over it. Brusca was working at the behest of capomafia Totò Riina, the very boss who had systematically made "excellent cadavers" of the many judges and politicians near Falcone. Now it was Falcone's turn. Riina's men were attempting their most ambitious crime yet.

Two rose marble obelisks, one facing each direction of traffic, stand as stark reminders of Judge Giovanni Falcone's sacrifice in the fight against the Mafia. In the most ambitious of the of its assassinations, a bomb detonated beneath the freeway killed Falcone, his wife and three bodyguards: Highway A29.

Palermo boss Salvatore Cancemi had planned the logistics and chosen the locations. Riina's brother-in-law Leoluca Bagarella supervised the eighteen-man operation. The explosives had been tested on Mafia land and speeds checked during rehearsals on the highway. Recent budget cuts left the route free of the helicopter patrols that had always preceded Falcone's convoy. The conspirators knew that the judge routinely spent weekends at the Palermo apartment he shared with his wife, Francesca Morvillo.

Spies watching the building from a nearby butcher shop, owned by a Mafia clan, learned that Falcone's visits were always precipitated by bodyguards retrieving the judge's white armored Fiat Croma to meet him at the airport. Brusca and company waited on the hill above Capaci the first three weekends of May 1992, but on the fourth Saturday, May 23, they got the message from the butcher shop: Falcone was flying home. Two men stationed at the airport sent word upon his arrival.

The government plane carrying the judge landed at the airport at 5:45 p.m. Francesca had been in Rome that week and was accompanying him on the trip home. Seven bodyguards stood by on the ground with the armored Croma and two other official cars. Upon landing, Falcone decided to drive. His bodyguard Giuseppe Costanza was made to take the backseat. The motorcade sped onto the highway to Palermo. The white Croma rode between the two police cars, also Cromas. At 5:58 p.m., they reached the Mafia's trap. The vehicles approached Capaci at a speed nearing eighty-seven miles per hour when Falcone ripped Costanza's key from the ignition and inserted his own. The car slowed to fifty-six as it glided over the culvert containing the bomb. At that precise instant, Brusca, watching through binoculars from the hill, pressed the button of his remote device. An enormous blast blew the highway wide open and imploded the center car, crushing the organs of Falcone and his wife. The lead car shot skyward and landed in a field two hundred feet away. The occupants all died on the spot.

Chunks of wrecked metal and asphalt rained on the ten-foot-deep crater that gaped forty-six feet across. Giuseppe Costanza, Falcone's driver consigned to the backseat, would be permanently disabled. The rear car had taken the least impact and its four escorts survived with injuries. A farmer who had witnessed the explosion rushed over to pull the Falcones from their car. The victims were soon loaded into emergency vehicles that had to wend through Palermo's thick traffic to reach the hospital. Judge Paolo Borsellino arrived in time to see the life pass out of his dear friend and colleague. Francesca died later that night despite two emergency surgeries. The news of Falcone's assassination threw Italy into shock. Sicily shut down in a general strike and, during the funerals, the streets of Palermo filled with angry citizens. Screams and insults met the government officials from Rome who pushed through the angry mob to enter the service in the Church of San Domenico. The tearful young widow of one of the escorts stood in mourning black at the pulpit next to a priest and addressed the crowd: "I, Rosaria Costa, widow of the agent, my Vito Schifani . . . ask that justice be served now. Turning to the men of the Mafia, because they are here inside . . . you know that for you there is the possibility of forgiveness. I forgive you, but you must get down on your knees—if you have the courage to change! But they don't change, they don't want to change."

The widow's wavering pleas gave voice to ordinary Italians fed up with the growing list of murder victims. People began to cast off their fears and take a public stand against the Mafia. Bedsheets painted with slogans calling out the Mafia hung from balconies across Palermo. Opposition groups formed to pressure the state into passing tougher laws against organized crime. With help from the FBI, investigators traced the DNA on fifty-three cigarette butts dropped at Capaci to Giovanni Brusca, who, after his 1996 arrest, admitted to having pushed the detonator. Totò Riina and other principals of the crime were sentenced with him. Several regretful accomplices later helped prosecutors recreate the timeline of the evil catastrophe. But a despairing sense of betrayal still haunts the marble halls of the Palace of Justice where Falcone worked. Numerous figures and rumors of figures fade in and out of judicial scrutiny. To conjure just one, witnesses described a secret government agent as a cocaine-sniffing mole with access to personnel files in the prosecutor's office. Said to have the "face of a monster," he has been pegged at the scenes of both Falcone's 1989 murder attempt and the Capaci massacre. And at another spectacular assassination to follow—that of Paolo Borsellino.

PART TWO

CORLEONE AND THE INTERIOR

ELEVEN
CORLEONE TO MEZZOJUSO

CORLEONE

BERNARDINO VERRO AND THE LITTLE BROTHERS

In the 1890s, a popular movement of landless peasants sprang from the miserable Sicilian outback. Calling themselves the Fasci—not to be confused with the later National Fascists—these workers' leagues occupied fields, called strikes, attacked city halls and burned records. Bernardino Verro, a tailor's son and the founder of the Fasci in Corleone, won contracts and reforms with the local landowners by leading a strike just before the harvest season of 1893. Traveling by muleback, Verro, a gifted orator, inspired Fasci groups to spring up across the interior. A proto-Mafia group in Corleone known as the Fratuzzi—the "Little Brothers"—took an interest in Verro, whose success as an organizer made him a marked man. A simpatico "brother" approached Verro and promised him protection and political solidarity. Accepting the offer with this influential, if nebulous, lodge, the naive leader soon found himself surrounded by the mafiosi of Corleo-

As Corleone mayor Bernardino Verro climbed the steps of the street (top) that led to his house, he was struck by eight bullets. After he fell, an assassin fired four more into his head: Via Bernardino Verro.

ne, participating in a mystic rite. His right index finger, bloodied by a pinpoint, was wiped across a paper drawing of a skull. As the image was burned by candle flame, Verro repeated the oath of an initiation that would remain secret until after his death.

Political backlash soon brought persecution to Verro and the Fasci. Prime Minister Francesco Crispi sent army troops to Sicily to crush Fasci demonstrations across the island. They did, within two weeks, but at a cost of eighty-three lives as soldiers opened fire on crowds in Palermo. The Fratuzzi, whose intention all along had been to manipulate the peasant movement for selfish gain, sided with the military and the property owners. Verro was interned in prison twice before the turn of the twentieth century. He traveled abroad to avoid further prosecution and to preach his political message. Returning to Corleone in 1906, Verro established the Agricultural Union to help farmers take advantage of the liberal new land reforms passed in Rome. The cooperative was granted several land leases for its farmers. But a competing organization, infested with Fratuzzi and corrupt clergymen, stood in opposition. Verro organized a tax strike against Corleone's crooked Catholic mayor, in 1910, and sank his administration. The Fratuzzi reacted: someone took a potshot that grazed Verro's arm and blew the hat off his head. Unshaken, he collared a Mafia boss and scoffed, "This time your boys only made smoke."

Convinced by his supporters to run for mayor of Corleone in 1914, Verro won a landslide victory and led a Socialist sweep of the city council. But the Fratuzzi struck again. On the wet afternoon of November 3, 1915, as Verro climbed the muddy steps of the street that led to his house, he was struck by a bullet shot from a stable. He managed to draw his pistol and fire off a return shot before seven more bullets hit him from two directions. After he fell, one of the assassins walked up and fired four more into his head. Years earlier, Verro had told a journalist, "If you only knew the crimes of these bullies who go unpunished!" No one has ever been charged with his murder.

NAVARRA AND LEGGIO: MEDIC VS. MANIC

Nothing less than complete sovereignty over Corleone would satisfy Michele Navarra, the Palermo-trained physician of the town's society set. This imposing doctor started a new Mafia from scratch by ratting out the old bosses to Fascist authorities. The wretched young men of the town were willing recruits to work his black markets. Thanks to the help of a cousin who had fought as a soldier for both the US Marines and Lucky Luciano's mob, Navarra was given the sole right to claim surplus vehicles left by the Allies at the end of World War II. The resulting bus system he established is still in use today. Among the doctor's exploitable resources was a local cattle thief he hired to perform his dirtiest deeds. Luciano Leggio, a cocky twenty-year-old from poverty, had become Sicily's youngest estate guard by shooting the old one down then applying for the dead man's job. But that wasn't the fiery upstart's first homicide: a year earlier, Leggio hunted

Dr. Michele Navarro was the director of the former Ospedale dei Bianchi (top), in Via Ospedale, as well as the town capomafia. His nameplate is still affixed to a pew in the Church of San Martino: Piazza Giuseppe Garibaldi.

down a policeman who had thrown him in the lockup for stealing wheat. A gifted gunslinger, Leggio became Navarra's favorite killer.

Dr. Navarra's prestige grew with his appointment to the directorship of the hospital in Corleone. "*U Patri Nostru*," they called him, "Our Father," the honorable doctor whose ring they kissed, the godfather of many of the town's kids, the kind practitioner of pro bono work. But the favors came at a price—especially for the politicians he put into office. On election day, Navarra issued certificates to hundreds of Corleonese voters stating they had been struck blind, requiring the assistance of his men to "help" mark the ballots properly. In truth, the citizens of Corleone were deathly afraid of Navarra. 153 people were killed on the streets of Corleone between 1944 and 1948 as the last vestiges of the old Mafia fell to the doctor's exterminators. But Leggio the hit man wasn't a simple follower of orders. He had cleverly infiltrated the meat markets of Palermo, on the side, with the cattle he stole and butchered. The young gun also opposed Navarra's intention to block the building of a dam that would submerge croplands and divert the water to Palermo. Navarra and neighboring bosses strongly opposed the project that would bring an end to the their irrigation monopoly. But Leggio salivated at the idea of controlling the construction contracts. He demanded that one of Navarra's men, an owner of vineyards and wheat fields, support the dam as well. When the farmer refused, Leggio smashed his wine casks and stole his wheat. Navarra was furious when he heard of his underboss's impudence. He ordered a hit squad to get rid of Leggio. When the shooters failed, having only wounded him, they ran away in fear.

Luciano Leggio had Navarra killed in order to become the new ruler of Corleone. Leggio lived at Via Lanza, 2.

Leggio's response to the murder attempt was swift. On the sweltering afternoon of August 2, 1958, Navarra rode along a backroad, driven in his Fiat sedan by a fellow doctor. A small truck darted in from the side and blocked the way. The car smashed into it. The unarmed Navarra screamed at the truck driver just as an Alfa Romeo raced up from behind, sandwiching the sedan. It was Leggio's car. Assailants jumped from the back of the truck and fired machine guns at the doctors, joined by the driver of the Alfa. A hail of 124 bullets hit the victims' heads and bodies and reanimated the vehicle to roll off the road. Luciano Leggio was suddenly the ruler of Corleone, a town dubbed Tombstone for the daily street skirmishes with Navarra's surviving faction. In the succeeding years, Leggio spent most of his time on the run, in and out of the law's clutches. A tuberculosis of the spine kept him laid up in various private clinics across Italy, even as he engineered his Palermo takeover. He was finally brought to justice for Navarra's murder in 1974, and he remained in prison for good. From his cage at the 1983 maxi-trials, the still cocky Leggio puffed on a Cuban cigar and told off the judges.

PLACIDO RIZZOTTO: HERO WITHOUT A BODY

When his mafioso father went to prison, Placido Rizzotto was left in charge of six siblings and the family cows before his twelfth birthday. His bed was a mat of straw. Rizzotto left Corleone as a Fascist soldier drafted to fight in northern Italy. But after Mussolini's fortune reversed in 1943, Rizzotto joined the partisans battling Nazis in the region. He returned home radicalized. "The rich," he said, "suck the blood of the poor and put the money in the bank." Before long, Rizzotto was leading masses of landless farmers into the countryside, planting red flags on the the estates controlled by Dr. Navarra and his enforcer Luciano Leggio. Leggio was known to attack

A bust in front of City Hall commemorates slain trade unionist Nicolo Rizzotto: Piazza Giuseppe Garibaldi.

farmers who opposed him by killing their animals and burning their barns. Rizzotto was unfazed: "Let them kill me. I'll have lived longer than a pig." He frequently denounced Leggio in public speeches and never shied from a confrontation. One account tells of a brawl in the park with Leggio that left the ruffian hanging by his coat on a spiked gate. One of Rizzotto's friends recalled that the Mafia "saw he was a real threat."

Rizzotto's only official post was that of secretary of the local union hall from which he emerged with two friends on the evening of March 10, 1948. En route to a meeting set up by Dr. Navarra, supposedly to discuss a land matter, he was approached by two men, one of whom was a childhood friend. After a short chat, a pistol was produced. "Let me go!" shouted Rizzotto as he fled up the steps of an alley. The men overtook him and threw a blanket over his head. They forced him into the trunk of Leggio's waiting car. A jailhouse confession by a former consort of Leggio eventually led to the capture of the two abductors and a warrant for the boss. The arrests were handled by police captain Carlo Alberto Dalla Chiesa, newly arrived from the north. The detainees each confessed their role in the crime: they had delivered Rizzotto to Leggio, who shot him to death and dumped his body in a deep crevice in the mountains.

The two prisoners took Dalla Chiesa and a search party to the rocky heights of the Rocca Busambra—a regular dumping ground for Leggio's victims. With the aid of the fire department, a policeman was lowered from a pulley into the hole. He emerged with the remains of three bodies and clothing recognizable as Rizzotto's. At the 1950 murder trial, the kidnappers retracted their confessions, claiming horrendous interrogations involving dungeons, fists and boots. As in most Mafia cases of the time, the suspects were acquitted for lack of evidence. Leggio's arrest warrant was cancelled. The sole witness to the killing, a thirteen-year-old shepherd's son, reported it to the wrong party. Sleeping with the flock in a field below the Rocca Busambra, he was awakened by a noisy struggle of men that ended in murder. The boy, traumatized, was checked into Dr. Navarra's hospital where he was, according to the autopsy, euthanized with poison. The only other person to come forward, a witness to Rizzotto's kidnapping, did so only in 2005—he was still too fearful to give his full name. Half a century after the killing, experts finally confirmed that some of the blackened bones plucked from the earth were Rizzotto's. In 2012, a team of forensic specialists positively matched his DNA.

TOTÒ RIINA: BEASTLY BOY

The gimpy, diminutive Luciano Leggio took over Corleone with the help of his younger mates: the mafioso Bagarella brothers, sure-shot Bernardo Provenzano and Leggio's chief hatchet man, Totò Riina. When a member of Dr. Navarra's defeated gang extended a hand in peace, Riina shot him in the face. Violence marked Riina's childhood from the age of thirteen, when his father and brother blew themselves up trying to defuse an unexploded American bomb. His murder habit began at nineteen. As Palermo deputy Vito Ciancimino would comment, "That man's got a revolver instead of a head." The Riina home reflected the hardscrabble life of Sicilian peasants in the 1930s. The living quarters for his family of nine doubled as the stable for farm animals. Crude wooden beds for furniture were contained in the cold stone walls under a broken-tiled roof. Totò, the stout "Short One," who struggled to write his own name, rejected the only two legitimate career paths available to boys of rural poverty: school or hard labor in the fields. Instead, he chose Mafia as a third and most likely way out of a miserable fate. The fortuitous friendships in this pack of delinquents, shaped by Sicilian traditions of resistance and force, created a Corleonese monster that defined the Mafia of the late twentieth century. Riina, whose star rose after Leggio's incarceration, literally killed his way to the top and waged an apocalyptic war on the Italian state.

Totò Riina's childhood home (left) reflected the hardscrabble life of Sicilian peasants in the 1930s: Via Rua del Piano, 13. As a successful Mafia boss, he built a tawdry pink mansion. It now houses the Guarda di Finanza police: Via Salvatore Aldisio, 143.

TOTÒ AND NINETTA: THE FIRST FAMILY OF COSA NOSTRA

Totò Riina was twenty-six when he was smitten by a raven-haired mafioso's daughter who was half his age. He quickly took to courting Ninetta, the kid sister of his fellow thug, Calogero Bagarella. Riina waited for her every morning at the end of the dark alley where she lived and followed her to school in silence. Before long, the young lovers were Corleone's oddest couple: Riina practiced his dark arts while the bookish Ninetta bused to

Riina waited for Ninetta every morning at the end of the dark alley where she lived: Via Scorsone, 24.

Palermo University daily—tailed by police—on the path to becoming a school teacher. Accused in 1971 of being a conduit for fugitive bosses, the twenty-seven-year-old Ninetta was declared guilty of Mafia association—a first for a woman—and put under surveillance in Corleone. She soon skipped town to live on the lam with Riina for the next twenty-three years, long enough to marry him and birth two boys and two girls. By 1990, the family was enjoying a life of cloistered luxury in an exclusive villa in the middle of Palermo. The capomafia showered his wife with jewels and furs. But the kids had to attend school under false names.

After Riina's arrest in 1993, Ninetta had little choice but to decamp, with her four teenagers, to the family home in Corleone. Her brother Leoluca became a father figure for Ninetta's eldest, Giovanni. Coaching his nephew's first murder, Leoluca swelled with the pride of a father whose son had just scored his first soccer goal. Giovanni and his younger brother Salvatore opened a roadside business selling farming equipment, a seemingly innocuous enterprise until police discovered it was a front for money laundering and extortion. In her florid schoolteacher's prose, Ninetta sent a passionate defense of her family to a newspaper in 1996: "My children are considered guilty of having been born of father Riina and mother Bagarella, an original sin that no purification can ever redeem." Incensed that society demanded her sons denounce their father, she wrote, "The Commandment 'Honor thy father and mother' must be respected by all." Her letter was written in reaction to Giovanni's life sentence for the crime of four murders, including those of a husband and wife whom he'd shot down, in front of their two children.

In 2008, Ninetta sat in an idling black Mercedes, waiting outside the prison gates for son number two, the one called Salvuccio —"Bad Sal." He emerged in a snow-white puffer vest and pink shirtsleeves to the delight of the paparazzi. In and out of prison numerous times for extortion, Salvuccio shared his mother's persecution complex as he found himself unwelcome from Corleone to Venice. "I say only that I have paid and I want to work," he griped to one reporter. "Apart from that . . . I'd like to see my father again, and to go see my brother Giovanni in prison." These words were in keeping with the Riina tradition that no family member denounce another.

UGO TRIOLO: DEATH AT THE DOOR

Ugo Triolo, a respected lawyer with a practice in neighboring Prizzi, lit up a smoke as he walked his black poodle in the chilly January air. When he got home, he pushed the intercom button so his wife would let him in. That's when he heard someone calling his name from the end of the dark street, "Ugo! Ugo!" He spotted a figure pointing a pistol at him. Six gunshots rang out. Triolo's wife opened the door and screamed as his lifeless body nearly fell on top of her. The lawyer's eighteen-year-old son arrived at that moment to find his father dead. The question of

Attorney Ugo Triolo's wife opened the door and screamed as his lifeless body nearly fell on top of her: Via Cammarata, 49.

precise motive troubled the police years after the conviction and sentencing of his Corleonese executioners. The bureaucrat had no criminal dealings with the Mafia. One theory rested on a rumor that Triolo held a large tract of land that he refused to sell. As one informer barked, "He should do what his *paesano* says, not what the law says." Or the Mafia may have figured that he knew too much, suspecting that one of his clients, accused of cattle-rustling, spilled the operation to him. Perhaps Triolo showed "too much zeal" when he prosecuted the godfather Leggio for a petty crime. Or it was the abrupt manner in which he ejected bosses Totò Riina and Bernardo Provenzano from his office when they arrived to make demands. It was Provenzano who reportedly pulled the trigger on Triolo.

THE HUNT FOR BERNARDO PROVENZANO

The top news flash for April 11, 2006, "Mafia Godfather Captured," was beamed worldwide, accompanied by the image of a pale old man smiling serenely from the center of a moving storm of cops. Footage showed the world the crowd gathered at the gates of the Palermo police station, cursing the silent figure as he was rushed inside. Bernardo Provenzano, the Phantom of Corleone, was apprehended in the last place anyone expected to find him: his home town. The police nearly gave him up for dead after his common-law wife Saveria Benedetta Palazzolo came out of hiding in 1992 to take up residency in Corleone. It seemed the logical move for the Mafia widow, especially with two sons—Angelo, 16, and Paolo, 9—in need of schooling. Still, investigators kept a constant eye and ear on the three, rattling them frequently with overnight raids. Saveria and her brood weathered numerous humiliations with the help of Provenzano's relatives in town.

Investigators spent nearly a decade monitoring the godfather's family via phone taps and bugs. They picked up enough veiled references to determine that the boss was not only alive but probably living in Sicily. Provenzano's communiques were *pizzini*—tiny typewritten notes folded and taped to fit between fingers, then passed from hand to hand. He was Italy's most-wanted man, a brilliant criminal able to slip across the French border three times to treat his prostrate problems. Yet, he was wholly dependent on his immediate family and a handful of intimates for his basic survival. Carmelo Gariffo, the boss's favorite nephew, lived around the corner from Saveria. His son-in-law Giuseppe Lo Bue went into business with the teen-aged Angelo Provenzano to sell home appliances. But agents noted frequent visits

Saveria Benedetta Palazzolo, wife of fugitive capomafia Bernardo Provenzano, came out of hiding to take up residency in Corleone. An outdoor camera recorded the numerous visits of Giuseppe Lo Bue. Police were riveted by what appeared to be an exchange of dirty laundry for clean: Via Ubertino da Corleone, 10.

Lo Bue was paying to Saveria when she was home alone. An outdoor camera recorded his numerous comings and goings, always with a heavy bag in hand. Another camera planted in her television revealed that the bag contained clothing. The police were riveted by what appeared to be an exchange of dirty laundry for clean. Surveillance was stepped up.

Agents choreographed an elaborate dance around the bag in transit, gliding by in unmarked cars and monitoring hidden cameras wedged into Corleone's ancient alleys. They tailed the laundry as it was couriered by car from Saveria to Giuseppe Lo Bue, then to his father Calogero, who entrusted it to another man in a car parked in the old town center. The license plate identified him as Bernardo Riina, a distant cousin of the imprisoned boss Totò. The last leg of the delivery was the most perplexing to police. Bernardo Riina drove the bag high into the mountain overlooking Corleone and out of view. Records showed that Riina owned no property in the vicinity. Agents set up telescopic lenses on another mountain miles away. The images, relayed to headquarters in Palermo, revealed that the bag's final destination was a modest sheep farm. Its owner, Giovanni Marino, was a farmer with a clean record, who received the visitors lined up every morning to buy his prized ricotta cheese and spring water.

To get a better view of the farm, officers of the select Catturandi squad moved in the dead of night to a spot just over a mile away. The stealthy operation, set up in a tiny shack, evaded even the binoculars of lookouts working on behalf of Provenzano. A waiting game began as the men focused on Marino's yard. They observed him adjusting a television antenna on the roof of an old cabin, one with a newly added compartment. The utility company confirmed that something inside the structure had been burning energy day and night since late 2004. On the morning of April 11, 2006, agents finally spotted a sign of life in the cabin. A ghostly hand emerged from the doorway and passed something off to Marino, who was lingering nervously.

Clockwise from top left: Carmelo Gariffo, Provenzano's mafioso nephew, lived around the corner from Saveria: Via Salvatore Aldisio, 6. Gariffo's daughter was married to Giuseppe Lo Bue, who was rarely home, as she complained in a marital spat captured on tape. Lo Bue relayed the bag of laundry to his father Calogero, who lived up the street: Via Salvatore Aldisio, 54. Calogero passed it to Bernardo Riina, a cousin of imprisoned boss Totò. Bernardo regularly delivered it to the mountain hideaway of Provenzano: Via 11 Aprile 2006 near Highway SS 188C. Note the add-on bathroom, built for the godfather, and the TV aerial.

The squad members wanted to strike, but the commander held off until Riina drove up the mountain with his package for the umpteenth time. Agents confirmed that he was delivering that same bag taken from Saveria. Riina placed it near the cabin door. The cameras panned away for a second then shot back to show the empty spot where the package had been. This was their moment.

"Go! Go!" the commander shouted. The team descended on the farm in a paramilitary blitz and burst through the cabin door. They were surprised to find an elderly man with a studied smile inside that squalid room. Bernardo Provenzano, on the run for forty-three years, was identified only by scars on his neck. Three crucifixes dangled from the necklaces he wore. A TV in his room broadcast the announcement that the Mafia godfather had been captured. Nearby was a cassette tape of *The Godfather Part II* soundtrack. The room was plastered with dozens of religious saints staring down as Provenzano was handcuffed. The added compartment, as it turned out, was a small bathroom. This capture was a banal finale for the walking death machine called "Binnu the Tractor," known to have killed dozens singlehandedly. Although a sum of $60,000 was found in a pile of underwear, and he controlled billions more, Provenzano had been living like a monk. On a table was a typewriter and several rolls of cellophane tape—materials used to compose his scripture-laced counsel in the *pizzini* that traveled to the far reaches of his empire. The ascetic boss warned his victorious captors, "You know not what you do."

THE CEMETERY OF CORLEONE

Clockwise from left: Dr. Michele Navarra's mausoleum towers over the graves of his many victims in the cemetery: Via Guardia. The remains of Bernardino Verro and Placido Rizzotto were placed in twin tombs in 2013. When Verro's old tomb was opened for transfer, workers found two skulls—an adult's, with a bullet hole, and a child's. The bones of Rizzotto were identified sixty-five years after his death.

FICUZZA

GIUSEPPE RUSSO: OUT OF THE WOODS

The mountain hamlet of Ficuzza opens onto a grassy piazza dominated by the gold-hued palace built by King Ferdinand III. Giuseppe Russo, lieutenant colonel of the carabiniere, kept his family in a little house on the piazza—a refuge from the hazards of his career as commander of the Mafia unit in smog-shrouded Palermo. The Calabrian native had a history with the bosses of nearby Corleone, having investigated their crimes. He

The piazza in Ficuzza is dominated by King Ferdinand III's palace (top). As Colonel Giuseppe Russo and Filippo Costa strolled the arcade, three or four men jumped from a car firing guns at them: Piazza Giuseppe Russo.

even discovered Totò Riina's honeymoon photo in a Palermo apartment. When threats were made, his superior, General Dalla Chiesa, mounted a symbolic counteroffensive by walking the streets of Corleone with Russo in broad daylight. After the great earthquake of 1968, centered south of Corleone, a flood of government funds was released. By 1974, hundreds of millions of dollars were available for the construction of the Garcia Dam. The Corleonesi tried to stake their claim by staging violent acts of intimidation, but Russo stood in the way of the contracts.

Russo stepped out onto the piazza on the evening of August 20, 1977, to meet his friend Filippo Costa. As they strolled the two-hundred-year-old arcade, a green Fiat 128 emerged from the dark forest road. It slowly cruised the length of the piazza then made a U-turn, stopping near the two oblivious friends. Three or four figures jumped out of the car and rushed Russo, firing .38s. One triggerman stumbled and fell on Russo before swinging a shotgun to his head and finishing him off. They killed Costa as well. As the assassins drove off, Russo's little girl ran out of the house to see her lifeless father lying in a pool of blood. A shepherd soon confessed to the murders and named two accomplices. All three were tried, convicted and sentenced, but these men were not mafiosi. The names of the real culprits were found in Russo's notes about corruption surrounding the Garcia Dam. The hit team had really been made up of Leoluca Bagarella, Pino Greco, Giovanni Brusca and Vincenzo Puccio, under orders from Riina and Provenzano. In 1997, sentences were handed to Riina, Provenzano and Greco for commissioning the murder of Russo. The shepherd and his friends were released after spending twenty years in prison.

MEZZOJUSO

PROVENZANO'S FREE PASS

A big, fat Mafia boss left prison in 1995 to spy for the police. Before his betrayal, Gino Ilardo answered only to his cousin Piddu Madonia, the undisputed head of Caltanissetta province. Ilardo—codenamed "Oriente" for his origins in the eastern city of Catania—was a trusted associate of fugitive Bernardo Provenzano. But now he was intent on helping the carabiniere to catch him. He alerted his police contact, Colonel Michele Riccio, to a secret summit Provenzano had arranged for October 31. It was a hazardous mission but it had a huge payoff: Ilardo would practically be leading Riccio by the hand to the elusive godfather. On the morning of the summit, Ilardo and the other mafiosi parked their cars at a crossroads outside Mezzojuso and walked away. The colonel's well-concealed men took down the license numbers and photographed the attendees while they awaited

Mafiosi parked their cars at this crossroads to attend Provenzano's summit. Colonel Michele Riccio's men recorded the license plates: Highway SS 121 at Road SP 55.

the orders from Rome to follow them. The undercover Ilardo was taken to a farmhouse where Provenzano received each man individually. As "Uncle Binnu" hashed over urgent matters—Totò Riina's war of terror and Giovanni Brusca's design to take over southern Sicily—a jittery Ilardo expected the carabinieri to break down the door at any second. But the raid never came and Provenzano adjourned the summit without suspicion.

As Colonel Riccio stated in his court deposition of 2001, "I was going to stop Provenzano, but the ROS (Special Operative Group) gave me neither the means nor the orders to do so." He said that his superior in Rome, General Mario Mori, "showed no signs of interest in what I proposed." Even when given explicit directions to the farmhouse, ROS colonel Mauro Obinu claimed it had been impossible to find, despite what Riccio described as its "conspicuousness." Riccio's account touched off several years' worth of trials to determine whether Mori and Obinu deliberately passed up a golden chance to net Provenzano. All along, Mori contended that Riccio's version was "riddled with inconsistencies" and tried to sue him for slander. But the charges stretched beyond the ROS brass. At the officers' trial, Riccio testified that "Provenzano had established contact with a member of Berlusconi's Forza Italia entourage . . . so soon, everyone would have to vote Forza Italia." He also stated that Mori had ordered him to forget the matter of political collusion. The state's witness, Gino Ilardo, had already told General Mori about the involvement of Berlusconi and his operative, Marcello Dell'Utri, in a May 1996 interview. Eight days later, Ilardo was shot dead in front of his Catania home by two assassins on a motorcycle. The job had been ordered by Ilardo's powerful cousin, Piddu Madonia. In July 2013, the ex-ROS officers Mori and Obinu were acquitted of aiding and abetting Provenzano, much to the dismay of the anti-Mafia movement.

TWELVE
BISACQUINO TO SUTERA

BISACQUINO

VITO CASCIO FERRO: ORIGINAL GANGSTER

If Don Vito Cascio Ferro didn't invent the *pizzo*, he helped to perfect it. Fresh from a jail sentence for kidnapping a baroness, the peasant-born strongman sailed to New York in 1901 and teamed with Giuseppe Morello, leader of that city's dominant gang. And thus the "Black Hand" of protection was introduced to the merchants of Little Italy. Morello's variation on the racket had simple terms: buy fake banknotes produced by his Sicilian gang in exchange for a trouble-free existence—or else. US Secret Service agents grabbed Cascio Ferro and charged him with counterfeiting. But it was just one of the sixty-nine arrests in his lifetime that would end in dismissal. The messy murder of one of Cascio Ferro's New York competitors put detective Joe Petrosino on his trail. The 1904 imbroglio ended in Palermo with Petrosino dead and Cascio Ferro off scot-free. The mafioso returned to the Sicilian town of his youth, Bisacquino, where he had distin-

From his house in the center of Bisacquino (left), Vito Cascio Ferro oversaw a crime network that stretched back to New York: Piazza Triona, 10. He always had enough cash to gamble away at the social club across the piazza.

guished himself as a cattle rustler and extortionist on the one hand and an Anarchist organizer on the other.

His gang days behind him, Cascio Ferro settled into the role of Sicily's preeminent—some say first—godfather. The iconic image of the elegant "man of honor" can be traced directly to Don Vito. From his house on the piazza of Bisacquino, this padrone arbitrated the disputes of villagers, receiving a kiss on the hand in appreciation. A local kingmaker and a dispenser of violence as a last resort, the don continued to oversee a crime network that stretched back to New York. Whatever the source of his income, he always had enough cash to gamble away at the social club on the piazza. Don Vito's perennial evasion of prosecution ended with the rise of Mussolini. A police sweep led by the Fascist prefect Cesare Mori in May 1926 took 150 criminals into custody, including Don Vito. His seventieth criminal charge since the turn of the century, for another old murder, was the one that brought him down. Bounced from prison to prison, he remained confined until his dying day in either 1942 or 1943, depending on whom you ask.

SANTO STEFANO QUISQUINA

LORENZO PANEPINTO: FIELD VISION

A marble plaque praises the work of Lorenzo Panepinto above the doorstep (left) where he was killed: Via Lorenzo Panepinto, 21. Four thousand mourners followed his coffin to the cemetery: Contrada Prisa.

Lorenzo Panepinto was a respected man of letters and a painter, a Socialist theoretician and an elementary schoolteacher. He took special interest in the struggle of the Sicilian peasantry and entered politics in 1889. He served on the city council of his native Santo Stefano Quisquina until Italy's conservative government stepped in to block his progressive majority. Like his friend Bernardino Verro of Corleone, Panepinto established a local chapter of the Fasci, in 1893. This workers' league disbanded after a few months, however, under the violent repression of

Prime Minister Francesco Crispi. Several of the group moved to Tampa, Florida, where they continued their organizing efforts and even sponsored Panepinto on an eight-month tour of America in 1907. The biggest gain for Sicilian Socialists of the early twentieth century came not at the ballot box but in the fields. A system of "collective rents" that Panepinto helped implement allowed farmers to manage the land themselves, bypassing the mafioso leaseholders altogether. The Mafia responded in its traditional manner. As Panepinto stood socializing at the entrance of his house, on the evening of May 16, 1911, he was shot twice in the chest and killed. His wife and three small children were left destitute. Black-veiled women howled for vengeance as four thousand mourners followed Panepinto's open coffin to the cemetery. But no score was settled and no justice brought solace. One woman, who had witnessed the event, bravely named Panepinto's attackers. The trial opened in March 1914 and a Mafia field guard stood accused. Yet despite the plaintiff's strong standing, Panepinto's widow withdrew from the trial "to exclude the possibility of a misunderstanding"—and, no doubt, grievous harm. The jury found the field guard not guilty.

THE MAD MONKS OF SANTA ROSALIA

It's hard to imagine that the serene environment at the hermitage of Santa Rosalia was ever a setting of depravity and violence. The woodlands surrounding the eighteenth-century abbey, built near the cave of Palermo's fabled saint to house an order of Benedictine monks, were emptied of bandits long ago. But in 1922, inside the convent, Brother Bernardo was slaughtered like a beast with sixty thrusts of a knife. A few mafioso monks of the hermitage, led by Friar Antonio Mortellaro, were put away for

For many years, the eighteenth-century hermitage of Santa Rosalia and its surrounding woods were scenes of depravity and violence: Road SP 24.

the murder of this father superior. The brotherhood fell apart. Harsh winters and food shortages drove the survivors to cattle rustling and banditry. Church authorities ordered the community to dissolve in 1928, but the monks stayed on, turning the hermitage into a refuge of bandits and mafiosi. It took Monsignor Giovanni Battista Peruzzo, inaugurated as the bishop of Agrigento in 1932, to impose order. He put two of the remaining priests in charge—a measure the monks resented. A few years later, Antonio Mortellaro returned. Freed from prison, the deposed friar brought chaos back to the abbey. The bishop sent in the police and Mortellaro was sentenced to six years imprisonment as "a bad person capable of any crime." Meanwhile, Monsignor Peruzzo came to be known as the "the bishop of the peasants." Though a fervent anti-Communist, he supported laws to split up the large estates to benefit poor farmers, earning him the ire of the Mafia and its landowning clients.

After the war, Monsignor Peruzzo occasionally forsook the

summer heat of Agrigento for the cool forests of Santa Rosalia. It was during one such forest retreat, on a walk with a priest, in July 1945, that Peruzzo was attacked. Three bullets were fired from behind a nearby bush. One pierced his lung and another struck his forearm. As he fell, three assailants with a smoking Italian army musket ran away. Peruzzo hobbled back to the hermitage, with the aid of his companion, sure of his impending death. He gave a confession then collapsed into bed while the cook ran for help. After a successful operation by a top surgeon of the region, the bishop was allowed to return to Agrigento to convalesce. An almost hysterical consternation spread. The devout fell to their knees outside his palace and prayed. The abbess of the Benedictine cloister in Palma di Montechiaro offered a sacrifice: ten of her youngest nuns would be locked up and starved to "give up life to extend that of their beloved pastor." Monsignor Peruzzo accepted and recovered fully to remain as diocesan until he died, at eighty-two, in 1963. Though no corporeal evidence of the heinous barter exists, the details were mentioned in a letter, sent to Peruzzo in 1956, written in dead earnestness by the abbess herself. As for the bishop's would-be ambushers, police named the villainous Antonio Mortellaro and two of his mafioso ex-monks. Whether they had tried to avenge Peruzzo for their expulsion or had acted in the political interests of the Mafia, they disappeared into the woods on the day of the shooting, never to be seen again.

LERCARA FRIDDI

LUCIANO AND SINATRA: TWO LUCKY GUYS

At the height of his stardom as a singer and actor, Frank Sinatra was photographed hanging out with mafiosi—Carlo

Gambino, Paul Castellano and the Fischetti brothers—but he didn't know they were gangsters. At least that's what he told the New Jersey State Commission's investigation of organized crime. Intimates of Sinatra claimed otherwise, pointing up his close friendship with Charles "Lucky" Luciano, in whose confiscated address book was listed the home of the entertainer. Strangely, the families of both men once lived on the same street in Lercara Friddi, a town known for sulphur mining and Mafia. Luciano was born there in 1897 with the name of Salvatore Lucania. The family's move to New York's Lower East Side when he was ten years old put him on a lifelong criminal path. He ganged up with tough Jewish kids like Meyer Lansky and Bugsy Siegel in their immigrant neighborhood. In the 1920s, Luciano and his "Young Turk" friends hustled and bribed their way to the top in bootleg booze and gambling, supplanting the old-fashioned Italian ma-

Clockwise from top: Lucky Luciano grew up in this house at Via Regina Margherita, 36. Deported from the United States in 1946, the celebrated gangster was feted by villagers in Piazza Duomo. Frank Sinatra's grandparents lived up the street from Luciano's family: Via Armando Duca della Vittoria, 6.

fiosi they called "Mustache Petes." Luciano used his power to establish the so-called National Crime Syndicate that defined the American Mafia for decades.

Deported to Italy in February 1946, after a ten-year sentence on a prostitution rap, police set Luciano loose back home in Lercara Friddi. The giddy villagers addressed him as "Excellency" and kissed his hand at a great feast they gave in his honor in the piazza. Sicily was essentially an extended stopover for Luciano. He went straight to work on guiding the old war-ravaged Cosa Nostra away from extortion and irrigation scams to the lucrative new world of narcotics. To that end, he stole away to Cuba in October 1946—an island strategic to his goals and a step closer to his American Mafia. But Luciano was spotted at Havana casinos palling around with Sinatra. He soon found himself back in the hands of the Italian police. Living out his days in Naples in relative luxury as a celebrity, he kept a thumb on the American syndicate and helped the Mafia corner the world heroin market. A US Senate Committee investigation of the drug trade "didn't make a dent in nothin' back in the States," observed the man they called Lucky. He died of a heart attack in 1962.

ROCCAPALUMBA

CESARE MORI: THE IRON PREFECT

Cesare Mori, Mussolini's man in Sicily, seemed stamped from the assembly line of the Fascist imagination. This former policeman from the north towered over most Sicilians in his tall black boots and tailored black suits. Prefect Mori adored the pomp of military ceremonies and wowed assemblies of townsfolk with high-flown speeches about workers and warriors destined to "shine forth forever amid the flash and lightning of legends and epics." In May 1926, following Mori's arrest of Vito Cascio Ferro, twelve hundred armed and mounted estate guards gathered on a hill overlooking the train station at Roccapalumba. A crowd of onlookers shouted *"Alalà!"*—the Greek battle cry—as horsemen arranged into martial formation. The liturgy was Mori's attempt to inspire a veneration of private property and, of course, an aversion to the Mafia. The official turned his back on the company so that those unwilling to pledge loyalty to king and country could leave. Every man stayed, shouting "I swear!" before signing the oath. Military music swelled and the recruits received Mass from an army chaplain at a makeshift altar.

Fascist prefect Cesare Mori inducted twelve hundred estate guards on the hill behind the train station: Highway SS 121.

Mori's ideological zeal made him an obvious choice for the job of top Mafia hunter in Sicily. Propaganda, he believed, would instill proper values in the populace, thereby freeing the island from the yoke of criminal rule. After Mori rounded up 130 suspected bandits and three hundred accomplices in the mountains, newspapers from Palermo to Milan praised his derring-do. Legend grew of "the Iron Prefect" and "the man with hair on his heart." The Duce wired his congratulations. Gangster Joe Bonanno wrote of Mori, "When it came to hunting down men, he did as well as any medieval grand inquisitor." The dreaded *cassetta* torture extracted confessions from the most innocent and resolute of men. The victim, strapped face-up to a wooden box, was whipped, electrocuted and de-nailed as his stomach was pumped full of saltwater. "And yet the judges," wrote Michele Pantaleone, "forced him to confess while he was still visibly suffering from the shock and before he had even realized that he was out of his torturers' clutches." Mussolini announced the death of the Mafia in 1928 and granted Mori a senatorial nomination. Menacing patrols of Blackshirts insured a ninety-two percent win. Yet the Fascist firebrand alienated local party officials who found it impossible to prosecute the eleven thousand low-level mafiosi he had arrested. Worse, the Mafia bosses had only grown in wealth and power since. Mori sent spies to follow his political enemies and accusations flew freely. Isolated, the great "Iron Prefect" was yanked from Sicily in 1929. He died a year before before the Allied armies landed.

VILLALBA

DON CALÒ VIZZINI: THE OPPORTUNIST

Despite a landing fraught with mishaps, the Allied invasion—codename "Operation Husky"—brought US and British armies to Sicily's southern shores in the earliest hours of July 10, 1943. The drive against Axis troops of Nazis and Italian Fascists on the island put liberators face to face with Cosa Nostra. As Mussolini fell, many local Mafia chiefs were tapped by unwitting commanders to fill the power vacuum. In Villalba, the mayoralty was given to Calogero Vizzini, known to the peasants who kissed his hands as Don Calò. The subliterate, rubber-featured Calò was an agrarian estate boss who had deftly manipulated the wartime black markets. He made a fortune thanks to his partnership with Vito Genovese, the Italian-American gangster who doubled as a trusted interpreter for the Allies. Though accused of dozens of murders and lesser crimes, Don Calò was

Clockwise from top left: the town square was the scene of Don Calò Vizzini's violent attack on his political opponents: Piazza Vittorio Emanuele. An inscription on Vizzini's tomb describes him as an "enemy of all injustices, a defender of the weak." The boss's chief detractor was surveyor and writer Michele Pantaleone, whose tomb is visible through mesh: Via Francesco Crispi.

reliably cleared with clergy support—he was related to the local priests. Villalba's piazza was bordered on the south by houses of the Vizzini family and on the north by those of the Pantaleones, the properties facing each other like the starting ranks of a chessboard. An enormous royal estate that surrounded the village was slated for government redistribution. It was also coveted by Don Calò. Michele Pantaleone, a young surveyor who supported the struggle of landless peasants, exposed the conflict in the left-wing press. The don struck back with an unsuccessful attempt on his life.

A postwar wave of activism caused a red scare that united the Mafia and the right-wing elites who wanted Sicily to secede and become an American annex. Don Calò, sniffing an opportunity to boost his authority with US backing, invited the Separatist leader Andrea Finocchiaro Aprile to propagandize the townspeople in the piazza. Pantaleone answered back by trucking in the Communist organizer Girolamo Li Causi a few weeks later. Before Li Causi's rally, according to Pantaleone, Don Calò treated the attendees to coffee in the village bar then warned them against disturbing the peace of Villalba. When Li Causi's speech broached the subject of the region's poverty, Calò shouted, "What you're saying is a lie!" The outburst was an apparent cue: a group of goons attacked the assembly with gunfire and hand grenades. Fourteen were wounded including Li Causi, who survived a shot in the leg. Calò denied involvement but sent apologies anyway. Within months he took control of the contested land. Though charged with ordering Li Causi's attack a decade later, the don was once again acquitted.

POLIZZELLO

FEUDAL FEUDO

The lay of the land in rural Sicily reflects its delayed exit from feudalism. Highland towns are former agrarian settlements separated by vast valleys. In the not too distant past, the upper class considered work a shameful thing. The ownership of land, but not its development, was the chief status symbol. A landowner derived income by leasing his estate, or *feudo*, to a mafioso middleman who, in turn, dumped all of the risk onto peasant subleasers. Even those farmers who were eventually granted land still had to pay rent to the Mafia, sometimes surrendering half of their crop. Despite the best intentions of the Italian state to ease southern poverty, land redistribution programs, on the books since the nineteenth century, were routinely tied up in red tape. Revolts in central-west Sicily erupted regularly as peasants demanded the breakup of large, undeveloped estates. Tensions increased in the periods after the world wars as thousands of Sicilian soldiers returned home to joblessness. Worker cooperatives were formed to obtain land allotments, a process requiring the use of savvy fixers to negotiate property transfers. Local godfathers like Calogero Vizzini and Giuseppe Genco Russo were perfectly suited to broker these deals, thus fulfilling the Mafia's traditional role as an intermediary. The co-ops became co-opted, as it were, but not by force or intimidation. The bosses themselves were the persuasive organizers of their own cooperatives, tipping the balance in their direction. Genco Russo contrived to become the sole authority on the royal estate of Polizzello, where he had shepherded as a boy. Hired as an overseer by the Princess of Trabia, the mafioso was authorized to handle a state-mandated land expropriation. Not only did he take control of the rents, he also kept a nice piece of acreage, illegally, for himself.

Godfather Giuseppe Genco Russo became the sole authority on the royal estate of Polizzello: Road SP 16.

MUSSOMELI

GIUSEPPE GENCO RUSSO: DANGER TO SOCIETY

On July 12, 1954, the citizens of Villalba gathered in church to pay their last respects to Don Calò Vizzini. Next to his cof-

Giuseppe Genco Russo assumed Don Calò's command. Shunned before his death, he was entombed in the family crypt: Road SP 17.

fin, amid a cloud of flowers, stood Giuseppe Genco Russo of Mussomeli, ready to assume Don Calò's command as ruler of the Sicilian Mafia. Genco Russo was the more violent of the two men, routinely brought up on murder charges only to be dismissed for lack of evidence. The unschooled boss never shed his rustic lifestyle. Even in wealth he kept a mule and an open-air commode of rock which, to the surprise of Mafia squealer Tommaso Buscetta, the don used during conversation. Genco Russo's reputation got polished up after the arrival of the Allied Military Government. Trusted as an ardent anti-Communist and a victim of Fascist persecution, Russo was put him in charge of civil affairs in Mussomeli in 1943. The following year, a court decreed him to be a "rehabilitated" citizen. He was anything but reformed: railcars filled with pasta left his mills to be sold on the Naples black market by New York gangster Vito Genovese.

At the 1957 Mafia summit hosted by Lucky Luciano in Palermo, an undercover cop overheard Genco Russo express misgivings about the mob's expansion into drug trafficking. "When there are too many dogs fighting over a bone," he said, "you're lucky if you can stay out of the way." Yet the godfather's very presence, many believe, was crucial to closing the deal with the American Mafia. Meanwhile, his prominence grew along with his wealth and he was frequently seen with business bigwigs and priests. As a boss from Trapani liked to say, "Did you see him in the newspaper today, that Gina Lollobrigida?" As with drugs so with politics:

Genco Russo followed the Mafia into the Christian Democrat party, winning a measure of legitimacy with his electoral win to the Mussomeli city council in 1960. In the anti-Mafia fervor following the Ciaculli massacre of 1963, however, he found himself in court for the first time since the war. Determined by a special tribunal to be "dangerous to society," the capomafia was banished to northern Italy on a five-year house arrest. He lived out his last lonely years back in Mussomeli, shunned by those who had respected him. Genco Russo died in 1976, at 83, denying to the end that he knew anything about the Mafia.

SUTERA

CALOGERO ZUCCHETTO: VESPA VIGILANCE

Calogero Zucchetto couldn't wait to leave his sleepy village of Sutera to become a cop. Before his twentieth birthday, he was on a team of bodyguards that escorted Judge Falcone through the streets of Palermo. He made the ranks of the Mobile Squad and quickly rose to become its star agent. Zucchetto worked alongside Beppe Montana and together they burrowed deep enough into the narco-world of Michele "the Pope" Greco to chart the Mafia's hierarchy. This information helped confirm the investigations of their superior, Vice Chief Ninni Cassarà. Greco and scores of his accomplices were dragged to trial. Chief Cassarà sent Zucchetto to Ciaculli, the heart of the Pope's operations, after receiving a tip that the fugitive boss Salvatore Montalto was seen in the vicinity. The agent worked on and off the clock, buzzing around the suburbs of southern Palermo on his little Vespa. He spotted Montalto with two hit men, Pino Greco and Mario Prestifilippo, which then allowed him to discover Montalto's hideaway home in Villa-

A bust of Calogero "Lillo" Zucchetto salutes his sacrifice as a Mobile Squad investigator: Piazza Calogero Zucchetto. He was laid to rest at the age of twenty-seven: Road SP 132.

bate. Montalto had betrayed his boss Totuccio Inzerillo to Totò Riina, dooming Inzerillo and gaining himself a seat on the Mafia Commission. He was also an essential link in a telephone chain that facilitated the transfer of drugs from Asia to South America and the US.

Joining the twenty-seven-year-old Zucchetto on one of his frequent surveillance missions, Chief Cassarà jumped on the back of his scooter and the two rode to Villabate, assuming the roles of carefree guys on a joy ride. They crossed paths with killers Prestifilippo and Greco, catching their attention. Prestifilippo recognized Zucchetto from the days when the undercover agent mingled with mobsters in Palermo. A few nights later, Zucchetto found Prestifilippo waiting for him outside his house. Zucchetto jumped into his car and the hit man did the same, pursuing him in a chase until he was shaken. "By now they've recognized me," Zucchetto told a colleague, "so they're already thinking of blowing me and my car to smithereens." Learning of the incident, Cassarà launched a raid on Montalto's house and captured him. Zucchetto was held back from the operation for his own protection. But it was too late. On the evening of November 14, 1982, Prestifilippo and Greco waited on a Vespa outside a bar in Palermo while Zucchetto dined inside. Once he emerged, a gun was drawn and five .38-caliber bullets were fired into his head. The killers sped off. (See the murder site on Page 32.)

PART THREE

THE WESTERN COAST

THIRTEEN
SALEMI TO PIZZOLUNGO

SALEMI

VITTORIO SGARBI AND THE MAFIA MUSEUM

The town of Salemi made headlines when its citizens elected controversial art critic Vittorio Sgarbi as their mayor in 2008. This curator, with a résumé of provocative exhibits across Europe, opened the Museo della Mafia in the old center in 2010. When Sgarbi resigned in scandal two years later, he left behind a world-class crime exhibit. Housed within a complex of cultural museums in an eighteenth-century Jesuit college, the elaborate multimedia spectacle addresses the Mafia from a variety of perspectives—historical, sociological and artistic, with a touch of Halloween spook-house fright. Upon entering, the visitor steps into a series of claustrophobic cabinets to experience radically altered environments. A tiled cubicle sickens with video imagery of shrieking animal slaughters combined with footage of Mafia carnage. A prison visitation booth leaves one confronting a mirrored self. Creative interpretations in various media—paint, ceramics,

Housed in an eighteenth-century Jesuit college, Mayor Vittorio Sgarbi's Museo della Mafia is a world-class crime exhibit: Via Francesco D'Aguirre, 8 (photo: Ronald de Grauw).

video—embellish an endless trail of actual newspaper covers with giant headlines and horrifying photos that tell, murder by murder, the story of Cosa Nostra. Mayor Sgarbi ignored a judge's order to remove one front page that depicted the arrest of Salemi natives Ignazio and Nino Salvo. The original complaint came from Nino's widow.

One of Sgarbi's first acts in office was to appoint Oliviero Toscani as Salemi's "Minister of Creativity." The shock-ad photographer, best known for his nude images of an anorexic model, seemed the perfect co-conspirator in a locale once a stop on the international narcotraffic circuit. But Toscani quit his post at the first whiff of Mafia, blowing the whistle on Sgarbi's chief political sponsor, Pino Giammarinaro. The politician, once aligned with deposed Sicilian governor Totò Cuffaro and Senator Andreotti's shadowy faction, had served a sentence for Mafia-related crimes. He was also considered the "godfather" of the healthcare system in Trapani province. Sgarbi's troubles with Giammarinaro began in 2010 over the allocation of assets seized from Salemi boss Salvatore Miceli, the fugitive drug lord captured in Venezuela one year earlier. The mayor resisted Giammarinaro's urging to give the money to one of his own charities. That's when the symbolic threats came. The head of a pig was delivered to the local police station. The carcass of a dog appeared near Sgarbi's office. Things came to a boil in May 2011 when authorities swooped in to seize $45 million worth of Giammarinaro's stolen assets. Though Sgarbi was not investigated for criminal acts, Salemi's city council was dissolved for Mafia association in 2012. The colorful figure promptly resigned, ran a failed mayoral campaign in Cefalù then left Sicily altogether.

PARTANNA

RITA ATRIA: THE TRUTH LIVES

They took her father when she was just eleven, then her older brother when she was sixteen. Rita Atria, the difficult daughter of a Mafia family, was full of wrath for the men of Partanna who settled their differences with sawed-off shotguns. She could not accept the fate of Mafia wives like her mother, who silently suffered under the laws of loyalty. Rita watched her sister-in-law Piera Aiello refuse that role.

Rita Atria abandoned the Mafia over the threats of her mother. Under the protection of Paolo Borsellino, the teen left home: Via Pergole, 24 (photo: Ronald de Grauw).

When Rita's mother finally visited her grave, it was to smash it to pieces with a hammer. The tortured woman, who died in 2012, now shares a new marker with her daughter: Via Castelvetrano.

Widowed at twenty-three by the murder of Rita's brother, Piera told the carabiniere what she knew about the Mafia of the region. Rita determinedly followed in Piera's steps over the mortal threats of her mother. The teen became a witness for the state in November 1991. Anti-Mafia magistrate Paolo Borsellino took an interest in the cases of Rita and Piera. He gave the young women a protective escort and moved them to Rome. But despite her new freedoms, and a new boyfriend, Rita felt doomed. She filled her diary with anguished thoughts: "I can't distinguish anymore between good and evil, everything has become so dark and squalid." Her sole source of security was Borsellino—"Uncle Paolo"—who, having daughters of his own, felt a kinship to the distraught girl.

But on July 19, 1992, Borsellino was killed in Palermo. The Mafia had once again stolen someone Rita loved. She despaired. She told Piera how she wanted her own funeral to be arranged, right down to the last flower. Piera was unable to cheer her. Then, on the afternoon of July 26, Rita stepped off the seventh-floor balcony of her apartment. A suicide note was found: "Now the one who protected me is no more, I've lost heart, I can't bear it anymore." Her funeral in Partanna was an all-female ceremony—even the pallbearers of Rita's white coffin were women—attended by activists of the burgeoning anti-Mafia movement. The only male who attended was the priest, but he made no mention of the Mafia and spoke only of sin. "Rita did not sin! She spoke out!" the women shot back. As she had requested, Rita was laid to rest next to her brother and away from her father. Her mother Giovanna stayed home with her face buried in a pillow. When she finally visited her daughter's grave, it was with a hammer in her purse. She took it out and pounded on Rita's marble photograph, smashing it into little pieces. "I love my daughter Rita," she told the arresting officers. Giovanna had made good on her threats to relatives to destroy the grave. The marker, inscribed with the words, "The truth lives," were chosen by Piera Aiello, the sister-in-law who'd inspired Rita to abandon the Mafia life. Rita's tortured mother appeared in court in 1993, silent and dressed in black, to accept a two-month suspended sentence for the desecration. In 2012, Giovanna was reunited with her daughter. She shares a new grave marker with Rita.

CASTELVETRANO

TURIDDU'S CAMERA-READY CORPSE

"Who is the bloodiest: the government that hunts me like a wild beast or I who defend myself?"

So asked the notices signed and posted by Salvatore Giuliano, pursued for the atrocities of the May Day massacre at Portella della Ginestra and other murders. With nearly thirty of his men captured—even his parents, brother and sister were behind bars—the bandit was keeping out of sight. Witness testimony later suggested that he was negotiating a secret exchange through a receptive government official: the bandit's extradition for his mother's freedom. The woman was released, in fact, in January 1950, followed by his brother. By July, some of the band's members were standing trial as suspects in the massacre. The Mafia was harboring Giuliano in a house in Castelvetrano belonging to a neutral party: a young lawyer named Gregorio De Maria. As the fugitive secretly hammered out details with a police captain toward a getaway to America, a trap was set by the carabiniere. Turiddu's bosom comrade Gaspare Pisciotta was persuaded to save his own skin by double-crossing his beloved friend.

The news of July 5 spread like fire across Italy. Salvatore Giuliano was dead, cut down, it was reported, in a gunfight with police. Front-page photographs showed the world-famous bandit lying face down and bloodied in the dusty courtyard of the house where he'd holed up. Next to him were a knapsack, a pistol and a Beretta submachine gun. The captain of the carabiniere fed the official explanation to legions of reporters on the scene. A secret informer, he announced, had guided his soldiers to the house where they were certain to find Giuliano preparing to flee the country. Under orders to withhold fire unless necessary, the troops were shot at in the night by two men from the house. After a forty-five minute firefight that discharged 190 rounds of ammunition, Giuliano lay dead in Mr. De Maria's courtyard.

Newspaper photographs showed the world-famous bandit lying face down and bloodied in the dusty courtyard of the house where he'd holed up. The incident was recreated on the site for Francesco Rosi's biographical film, *Salvatore Giuliano:* Via Fra' Serafino Mannone, 54.

The story was riddled with more holes than the deceased bandit. None of De Maria's neighbors had heard a lengthy exchange of gunfire—not even the two bakers next door who soldiers ordered off the street. Then there was Giuliano. Wearing only an undershirt, trousers and sandals, and carrying no money, he had seemed ill-prepared to embark on a long voyage. And the blood from his wounds had somehow flowed upward. It took a sharp journalist from Milan to piece together the most probable scenario. Under the headline, "THE ONLY CERTAINTY IS THAT HE'S DEAD," the story accurately guessed at Pisciotta's betrayal, his close-range shooting of Giuliano and the dragging of the body to the courtyard, where it was fired upon by police machine guns. While the mysteries surrounding the death of Turiddu may be argued over forever, the account in the Milanese news article was endorsed by three men involved: De Maria the property owner, Pisciotta, who admitted to shooting his sleeping friend, and the captain, who recanted his own false account that nevertheless remained the official story.

MATTEO MESSINA DENARO: DANGER DIABOLIK!

The wealthy godfather of Castelvetrano came to a freakish end. Francesco Messina Denaro—"Don Ciccio" to his subjects—was found dead by the side of the road, in November 1998, suited up in his Sunday best, saving morticians the trouble. During the funeral, protected by armed men, the priest warned that judging the capomafia was "a task that belongs only to the eternal Father." Thus began the Messina Denaro family death cult, a public mourning that included the widow-in-black's daily visits to Don Ciccio's tomb and annual newspaper obituaries laced with scripture or Latin verse. With his older brother Salvatore in jail, the reins of the Castelvetrano Mafia were passed to Matteo Messina Denaro, a flashy figure ripe for mythologizing. The champagne-swilling, Versace-adorned "playboy godfather," learned in both Cicero and *Donkey Kong*, was tagged with the nickname Diabo-

The Messina Denaro family death cult included the widow-in-black's daily visits to Don Ciccio's tomb: Via Aurelio Saffi.

lik, a super-criminal from the comics. The mafioso fantasized about installing pop-up machine guns in his Porsche. Standing in marked contrast to the conservative bosses of old, Messina Denaro was a ladykiller in every sense. He left behind a string of swooning mistresses—and strangled to death the pregnant girlfriend of an enemy. Sought, since 1993, for his involvement in the Mafia massacres of Palermo and mainland Italy—and dozens more murders—Messina Denaro's authority was gradually revealed after the arrest of his superiors. Bernardo Provenzano, taken in 2006, called him "Alessio" in his messages but addressed everyone else as a coded number. The incarceration of fellow aspirants Salvatore Lo Piccolo, Gianni Nicchi and Mimmo Raccuglia boosted Messina Denaro's profile. So did his connections with drug traffickers in Colombia, Canada, Germany and South Africa.

Although many of Messina Denaro's affiliates have been caught, he still remains at large as of this writing. The FBI wants him and Italian authorities have put up a $2 million reward for his capture. Yet authorities believe he enjoys a safe existence somewhere in his own Trapani province. One report put him at a 2010 soccer match, wearing the pink jersey of the Palermo team, during a meeting of the bosses. Celebrated in his home town as a job provider, the capo's web of influence covers the island. Much of his money was laundered through a chain of supermarkets and several wind turbine farms. In 2013,  a record $1.7 billion in assets were seized from the "Lord of the Wind," Vito Nicastro, a close associate. Messina Denaro's political protection and wealth both stem from the same source: his relationship with the powerful D'Alì family that stretches back to the days when Don Ciccio was a guard on the D'Alì estate. Senator Antonio D'Alì, despite standing trial for Mafia association, was reelected in February 2013 before being acquitted of the charge in September. Commenting on the elusive Diabolik, the tarnished politician said, "I hope this rascal is captured soon."

MAZARA DEL VALLO

MAZARA: SACRED AND PROFANE

The ancient seaport of Mazara del Vallo falls under the influence of Mafia families from both Corleone and Trapani. Gaetano Riina, brother of Corleonese boss Totò, owned Mazara property and was arrested there, and the local assets of Matteo Messina Denaro of Trapani were seized. In the 1950s, the harbor was a busy way-stop for boats transporting heroin, cocaine

Ex-convent, Piazza San Michele Arcangelo.

and hashish from North Africa to the US. Before he was taken into custody, trafficker Giuseppe Mancuso held meetings with his men in the nunnery of San Michele Arcangelo, where his sister was the mother superior.

LOCOGRANDE

ALBERTO GIACOMELLI: BAD MANNERS

Retired judge Alberto Giacomelli barely reached the end of the road bordering his property when he was shot dead: Via Falconara, 60.

With forty years on the bench behind him, retired magistrate Alberto Giacomelli enjoyed his autumn years farming the forty acres of his estate. The career of "Uncle Alberto," as the seventy-nine-year-old judge was fondly called, was remarkable only for its lack of incident in Mafia-plagued Trapani province. His hesitancy to make waves was the most confounding aspect of his murder on September 14, 1988. At 8 o'clock that morning, Giacomelli left his villa in his Fiat Panda to run an errand. He barely reached the end of the road bordering his property when he was blocked by a man on a motorized bicycle. The judge stepped out of his car and was immediately shot in the stomach and the head. His body was found in the middle of the road next to the Fiat, along with the bike and the gun, a Brazilian-made Taurus with the number scraped off. Only after two mafiosi later agreed to cooperate with justice was any light shed on the nasty business. Three years before his death,

Judge Giacomelli signed an order of seizure of a home in Mazara del Vallo owned by Gaetano Riina—an unpardonable offense against the Corleonese boss. Trapani godfather Vincenzo Virga was charged with ordering the death sentence—that is, until one of the court's collaborators went mum on the stand. Gaetano Riina's infamous brother Totò ended up taking the rap alone.

PALMA, NAPOLA AND VALDERICE

MONTALTO AND ROSTAGNO: DEATH IN THE STICKS

Two nights before Christmas 1995, prison guard Giuseppe Montalto was murdered in Palma, a dusty little crossroads near the salt fields of Trapani. Montalto had worked the cellblock at Ucciardone prison that held Cosa Nostra's most dangerous bosses. Sentenced under the tough laws of Article 41b, the men were furious.

The Mafia killed Ucciardone guard Giuseppe Montalto "as a Christmas gift to friends who find themselves in prison." Road SP 21, Palma.

41b restricts nearly all contact with the outside world, putting a crimp on conducting business from behind bars. The alert Montalto had intercepted three paper *pizzini* intended for Nitto Santapaola, eastern Sicily's most powerful boss, and turned them over to authorities. An order was issued by Vincenzo Virga, the capomafia of Trapani, to "kill a cop as a Christmas gift to friends who find themselves in prison." As an agent of the penitentiary police, Montalto was that cop. On the night of December 23,

Montalto and his family were just leaving the house of his in-laws. His wife and ten-month-old daughter were seated in the family car. As Montalto took his place at the wheel, two men in ski masks emerged from the blackness. Three shots were fired. He was killed by a single bullet in the face.

Two thousand mourners packed the tiny church where the funeral was held, but the criminal community was elated. When mafioso Giovanni Brusca wrongly attributed the precision killing to Matteo Messina Denaro and Vincenzo Sinacori, his fellow bosses basked in the compliment. But it was such precision that enabled the police to tie the incident to another crime that had occurred in the area seven years earlier: the assassination of Mauro Rostagno, a journalist transplanted from Turin. Rostagno was an authentic specimen of student rebellion that swept the world's universities in 1968. A founder of a radical group that promoted occupations and street clashes, he accepted a position in the sociology department at the University of Palermo in 1972. Rostagno founded a drug rehabilitation community he named Saman, a Hindi word meaning "song of praise." Three thousand young drug and alcohol dependents settled there and planted citrus trees in the quiet valley below Mount San Giuliano.

But the journalist in Rostagno could not ignore the blatant criminality overrunning the regional government of nearby Trapani. Facing cameras in the small television station he had established, he accused the city's political and business elites of Mafia collusion. Apparently, they were watching. On the evening of September 26, 1988, as Rostagno drove along the dirt road leading to Saman, he was hit by a barrage of bullets flying from cross directions. His windshield shattered and he received two fatal blows in the head and five in the body. The startled residents found their mentor on the blood-soaked seat, his head cocked back and staring in death. Ballistics experts noted that the cartridges used in both the Rostagno and Montalto killings had been overpacked with gunpowder to cause greater damage. Each man was struck long-range by assailants in the dark. And the same stolen Fiat Uno was at both scenes, torched after Montalto was slain. A reformed mafioso fingered Trapani councilman Francesco Orlando and hit man Vito Mazzara. Orlando was ultimately absolved, but Mazzara, a former trapshooting champion, was given a life sentence for the two killings, as was his boss Vincenzo Virga, confined under Article 41b.

As Mauro Rostagno drove along the dirt road leading to the rehab community he founded, he was hit by a barrage of bullets: Road SP 34, Napola. Though Torino-born, he is buried in nearby Valderice: Via del Riposo, 2.

TRAPANI

GIANGIACOMO CIACCIO MONTALTO: MEMBERS ONLY

"Isis 2," the Masonic Lodge whose member list included Trapani's leading professionals, politicians, judges and crime bosses, was the place to do business during the Mafia's go-go years of the early 1980s. At the time, Trapani province was awash in heroin

profits—Europe's largest refinery was located in nearby Alcamo—and this cabal had tied up the sectors of healthcare, sanitation and public works. It was the very picture of an efficient, institutionalized Mafia. Its only obstacle was a principled deputy prosecutor who knew everything about it. Lacking a bodyguard or even a computer, Judge Giangiacomo Ciaccio Montalto had sifted through bank records and uncovered a drug route to Montreal. He seized assets and brought several members of the local Minore clan to trial. But Ciaccio Montalto realized his own isolation when he heard a recording of a fellow magistrate arranging a bribe with a boss. After a defendant in a courtroom made a gesture at him to symbolize death, he put in for a transfer to Florence. In the meantime, he pursued his cases as aggressively as before. Shortly after 1 a.m., on January 26, 1983, Ciaccio Montalto stopped his Volkswagen Golf at the gate of his palazzo, where two or more men were waiting for him. Before he could open the car door, the judge was hit in the head and chest by seventeen rounds of a 7.65-caliber submachine gun and a .30-caliber Luger. He lay there dead all night, wedged backwards between the bucket seats, in the silence of the terrified neighborhood. At sunrise, a passerby discovered his bloody corpse and alerted the police.

SAN GIULIANO PRISON: ROOM SERVICE

Inaugurated in 1965, the San Giuliano Prison in the city of Trapani is neither old like Ucciardone nor new like Pagliarelli. But the guards seen sweeping the outer walls with bomb detectors indicate a Mafia presence. So, too, did a request for room service by some inmates in 2008. Four bosses of the Naples Camorra were caught on video slipping bribe money to a guard in exchange for champagne, lobster, caviar, mozzarella and Neapolitan pastries. The gang members had presented their shopping list to their incorruptible sentry, who swiftly took it to prosecutors and helped set up a sting.

San Giuliano prison: Via Madonna di Fatima, 222.

PIZZOLUNGO

BARBARA ASTA AND THE INNOCENTS

When magistrate Carlo Palermo uncovered an international drug and arms operation in the northern city of Trento, in the mid-1980s, a related bribery scandal erupted in Parliament. Certain higher powers apparently found this public servant a little too efficient and closed his investigations. Frustrated, Palermo transferred to Trapani to take the place of his murdered colleague, Judge Ciaccio Montalto. In those days, the northwest corner of the island hid a number of factories busily refining Turkish heroin for the American market. The thirty-eight-year-old judge arrived with a list of thirty or so mafiosi he had connected to trafficking and other crimes. Two weeks after his arrival, the Mafia threw him a welcome party. On the morning of April 2, 1985, Judge Palermo was being whisked down the coastal highway

A bomb meant for Judge Carlo Palermo instead exploded under the car carrying Barbara Asta and her sons: Road SP 20.

from a military base to Trapani in an armored Fiat 132. Following close behind were his bodyguards in an unprotected Fiat Ritmo. Waiting for them was a Volkswagen Golf, parked by the side of the road in the town of Pizzolungo. The car was empty except for nearly fifty pounds of TNT, set to detonate by remote control.

As Palermo and his escorts neared Pizzolungo, another car, a Volkswagen Scirocco, sped up to pass them. Thirty-year-old Barbara Rizzo Asta was at the wheel, racing to get her twin six-year-old sons to school on time. At the instant she overtook Palermo's 132, the car bomb exploded, heaving her Scirocco into the air and blasting its three occupants into a rain of body parts. Tiny feet fell in the courtyard of a house. An ear lobe hit a bed stand near an open window. Barbara's armless corpse landed three hundred feet away. By chance, her husband and her brother were the first to arrive at the chaotic scene, but they left without realizing that anyone they knew—least of all Barbara and the twins—had been killed. The boys' older sister Margarita was already in school at the time. On the day of the funerals, passing the death scene, the ten-year-old girl noticed a detail she'd never forget: a bloody patch on the wall. "My father explained to me that it was from the body of one of my two little brothers hurled against that house," she recalled later. "At that moment I was catapulted into the adult world." Margarita was shielded from the television news that followed, but she read the papers in secret. "They talked about the Mafia, drugs, billions of lire, of judges and murdered policemen. I would see the photos of Judge Palermo in his hospital bed, his hollow face, and I'd ask myself why. Why my mother, my little brothers? What did they have to do with this war?"

FOURTEEN
SCIACCA TO RACALMUTO

SCIACCA

ACCURSIO MIRAGLIA: RADICAL ROYAL

Accursio Miraglia was the wealthy descendant of Spanish-Sicilian nobility who married a Russian ballerina related to the czar. Ironically, his politics were influenced by the October Revolution of 1917, and he considered himself an Anarchist-Communist. Although he was booted from his bank post in Milan for "political incompatibility," Miraglia remained active in business upon returning to his native Sciacca. But when the Gullo law passed in 1944 that gave peasants the right to work neglected fields, Miraglia wasted no time starting a workers' cooperative and announcing his "cavalcade." They came by the thousands—ten thousand by one count—in September 1946: peasants on muleback, bicycles and foot. Miraglia's aim was to reassign five thousand acres of olive trees and two hundred thousand crops to the workers. His inspiration was a quote from Hemingway's anti-Fascist novel *For Whom the Bell Tolls*: "It is better to die on

Counterclockwise from top left: A plaque over the cul-desac where Accursio Miraglia lived marks his murder site: Via Orfanotrofio, 25. Peasants carried his coffin to the cemetery a week after his death: Via Cava dei Tirreni, 12.

your feet than to live on your knees." The cavalcade was a major offensive against the enforcers of this Mafia-infested terrain.

The bosses retaliated. On the night of January 4, 1947, Miraglia left his office on foot accompanied by two colleagues. As the men neared his house, a sudden volley of shots struck Miraglia and he fell dead. A young man with a shotgun was seen fleeing in the light of a streetlamp. Miraglia's companions convinced the police that the three enforcers had acted in revenge, and arrested them. As the suspected ringleader was escorted to the prison in Palermo, he claimed a sudden illness. The party stopped in Corleone and the detainee was checked into the local hospital, which was run by the town's capomafia, Dr. Michele Navarra. A staff physician diagnosed the man with blood loss due to a hemorrhage, an unusual diagnosis that allowed him to evade prison in favor of a stay in a Palermo clinic. The next day, that city's public prosecutor declared all the charges were dropped for lack of evidence. The three suspects were freed. In Sciacca, the body of Miraglia lay in state for six days. Peasants carried his coffin to the cemetery on the wet winter day that followed. "When he was murdered, everyone backed away and got frightened . . . and each tried to hide the fact that he belonged to our group," observed a member of the cooperative. "It was always like that for those killed by the Mafia."

LUCCA SICULA

PAOLO BONGIORNO: PARTY MAN

Unlike the blue-blooded Miraglia, Paolo Bongiorno came to his politics out of sheer desperation. Yet the two trade unionists' fates were strikingly similar. Bongiorno, born of penniless laborers in Cattolica Eraclea, took his wife and five children to live in Lucca Sicula, in 1949, a town as bleak as the one they had just left. The only work he could find was backbreaking and poorly paid. He joined the local Communist party and put his limited education to use. Bongiorno rose fast as a leader of strikes for better wages and shorter days. His activism made him poison to employers. Unable to support his family with sporadic work, he suffered a nervous breakdown in 1959 and was sent to a clinic in Palermo. A month's rest did him good so he resumed his duties for the party. His devotion was repaid: Bongiorno's name appeared on the slate of candidates for the Lucca Sicula city council in the 1960 elections. He had reached the point where he was a serious threat to the establishment and was seen being harassed by a pair of local

Candidate Paolo Bongiorno, a threat to the establishment, was killed in the streets. His tomb bears red flags. Road SP 35 near Via Retta.

mafiosi.

On the night of September 27, 1960, Bongiorno left the party office with his nineteen-year-old nephew. They chatted as usual as they walked through the quiet streets. A man waiting with a shotgun stepped around a corner and fired two shots into Bongiorno's back. He screamed in pain and stumbled forward, then fell to the ground. His nephew cried for help and made a dash to the Bongiorno house yelling, "Auntie, open up! They shot him!" The two of them, with help from her brother, carried Bongiorno home and laid him on the bed. He drank the glass of water his wife gave him, looked into her eyes and died. He was thirty-seven. Everyone in town knew it had been a political assassination. Bongiorno was often seen in the piazza arguing violently with Antonino Mulè, a local landowner. Yet dozens of people responded to interrogation with variations on the old Sicilian proverb, "He who speaks little lives a hundred years." The investigating marshal dusted off the old love triangle theory, declaring, "It's a feminine thing." Only the victim's family invoked the name of Mulè, who was finally put on trial in Sciacca. As in that city's Miraglia case, the suspect was dismissed for lack of evidence.

SICULIANA

THE CARUANA-CUNTRERA CLAN: MEET THE ROTHSCHILDS

Tiny Siculiana's contribution to the world was the export of brilliant gangsters. From its old rural Mafia grew one of the richest criminal empires in history. Countless members of the Caruana and Cuntrera families—so populous and intermarried they're known as a single hyphenate—invaded the Americas like conquistadors. The riches they derived from their Atlantic drug routes won them the label "the Rothschilds of the Mafia." Paving the way was Siculiana native Nick Gentile. "Uncle Cola," as he was called, set off for America in 1903 and became an early pioneer in heroin sales alongside Lucky Luciano. A Caruana—Carmelo—entered the scene in the 1950s, when he and a partner began supplying the illicit stuff by the suitcaseful to a friend of Uncle Cola in Palermo. From there it was smuggled to a Canadian mob for US distribution. Based on its success, the Siculiana clan was invited to join forces with Agrigento boss Giuseppe Settecasi, Luciano's dope supplier. It was a big step up in Cosa Nostra's ranks. A diaspora occurred in the 1960s and 1970s

From Siculiana's old rural Mafia grew one of the richest criminal empires in history. A nameplate representing the leading families—the Caruanas and the Cuntreras—is found in the Church of the Santissimo Crocifisso, Piazza Umberto I.

as various Caruana-Cuntrera members left Italy, some willingly, others by court order. Many went to Brazil and Montreal. Others to London and Venezuela. The locations were chosen to advance the business of drugs—heroin, cocaine and hashish.

During the 1980s' Pizza Connection, the Siculiana clan was a bridge between the Palermo Mafia and New York's Bonanno and Gambino families. Dummy import-export companies were set up while lavishly bribed authorities looked the other way. Masters at corrupting banks to launder its profits, the family acquired hotels, nightclubs and real estate—it practically owned the Caribbean island of Aruba. But the shock of the Palermo assassinations of 1992 precipitated a global Mafia crackdown. The Italian government and the US Drug Enforcement Administration together put the squeeze on Venezuela to chase the Sicilian drug lords from their fancy lairs. A trio of Cuntreras were caught and extradited, but Alfonso Caruana, son of the enterprising Carmelo, escaped to Canada. As a result of the organizational shakeup, the cocaine tycoon was now the family capo. Resuming affairs in a Toronto suburb, Caruana made daily rounds in a gold Cadillac, stopping at phone booths to arrange coke transfers. But his knack for invisibility was undone in 1995 at his daughter's wedding, a sumptuous Mafia reception under police surveillance. A trace of the guests' license plates yielded a great surprise: the elegantly tuxedoed father of the bride was the Siculiana family's number-one. Hunted by governments on three continents, Caruana had quite unexpectedly flown into a net.

CATTOLICA ERACLEA

GIUSEPPE SPAGNOLO: THE PEOPLE'S MAYOR

A bust depicts Giuseppe Spagnolo (left), who spent his time at City Hall working on behalf of poor farmers: Via Enna Palazzine Agricole. He is entombed in the cemetery next to his wife: Via Calvario.

The archpriest of Cattolica Eraclea refused the slain Communist farmer a funeral in the Lord's house. Even so, the procession stopped in front of the Church of the Sacred Spirit to pray for the soul of the Mafia victim. The peasants of the area had come to bury one of its leaders, Giuseppe Spagnolo, the former mayor of the village. The culprits were yet to be caught—one of them even marched to the cemetery arm-in-arm with Spagnolo's oldest son. Spagnolo had spent his time at City Hall instituting the government reforms passed on behalf of poor farmers. As the founder of the local workers' cooperative, he championed the takeover of lands belonging to a baron of the region. A pummeling by eight thugs and an arson attack on his house drove the activist to sleep away from his family. He slept on a bed of hay in the fields of his small plot, far from town. Worried when he didn't come home the morning of August 14, 1955, Spagnolo's wife and son set out for the fields. They found him, dead, lying where he had slept. He was full of shotgun wounds.

A mule with a distinctive brand brought about the arrest of a Rosario Gurreri. He confessed to having loaned the beast to three mafiosi he listed by name to assist in the murder of Spagnolo. During the trial, Gurreri's lawyers tried to paint the shooting as an "act of honor." Spagnolo, they claimed, had made improper advances on the mother-in-law of one of the aggressors. But testimony delivered by Spagnolo's widow convinced the court that the crime was a political assassination by the Mafia. Antonino Manno, local capomafia and adversary of Spagnolo, refused to testify. The three mafiosi Gurreri named were found guilty of the murder and sentenced in absentia: they had fled to Canada to be absorbed by its growing underworld of Sicilian expatriates. Gurreri was sent to prison as their accessory. Upon his release, four years later, he felt the lure of Canada as well. He changed his given name and bought part of an Italian restaurant in Montreal. One spring morning in 1972, as Gurreri prepped the kitchen, he was seized and hacked repeatedly with a meat cleaver in the face, head and neck. A hunting knife was left buried in his chest. The revenge killing showed that old Sicilian rules still applied in Montreal. And that the Manno family was still running the show.

THE RIZZUTO CLAN: MAPLE LEAF MOB

Whether done for love, business or both, Nicolò Rizzuto's marriage to the daughter of godfather Antonino Manno was a promotion for the young mafioso. Rizzuto, in turn, took the Manno dynasty global when he moved his family to Montreal in 1954. The city had been a boomtown ever since Corsican heroin producers —the "French Connection"—colonized the port in the 1930s.

Lesser crimes like gambling and the rackets were monopolized by the Cotroni family from Calabria, on the toe of Italy's boot. Even New York's Joe Bonanno claimed a piece of the city, through his Canadian delegation. The Bonannos struck a lucrative partnership with the Cotronis, but inevitable Sicilian-Calabrian tension grew into rivalry. As Niccolò—now "Nick"—moved up in the Bonannos' Montreal faction, he was joined by expat members of the Caruana-Cuntrera clan from his home region in Agrigento province. Soon the Sicilians were importing drugs into Montreal and selling them independently of the Calabrians. Rizzuto's little side business got under the skin of Paolo Violi, the boss who replaced capo Vic Cotroni when he went to jail. In his bid to take control of Montreal, Violi lobbied the New York bosses until he got what he wanted: a death sentence for Nick Rizzuto.

But Rizzuto was a step ahead. With a preemptive strike at Violi, Montreal became a shooting range. The weapon of choice was classic Cosa Nostra: a heavy shotgun. The first to fall was a trusted Violi aide, blown from the arm of his wife as the couple emerged from a showing of *The Godfather Part II* in 1976. The next year it was Violi's younger brother, blasted in the face and pistol-shot in the chest. Paolo Violi himself was executed in a sandwich shop in 1978 while playing cards. Reputedly kissed on the cheek by another player, the Calabrian chief was shot in the back of the skull. Finally, in 1980, the last surviving Violi brother was picked off in his kitchen by a sniper's rifle. Nick Rizzuto came out on top—for a while. In 1988, he was busted for cocaine possession in Venezuela and sent up for five years.

The 1980s saw the rise of Nick's son Vito Rizzuto, a lifestyle godfather of Montreal who had a fleet of luxury cars. Despite his connection to sixteen tons of hash seized in Newfoundland and the discovery of seven hundred grams of coke in his Venezuelan home, no charges ever stuck to "the Teflon Don." Not, at least, until 2004, when he was picked up by Canadian authorities and extradited to the US on a racketeering indictment. Vito also was held to answer for his secondary role in the 1981 massacre of a mutinous group of New York Bonanno bosses, as recreated in the film *Donnie Brasco*. Half teflon, Vito served five years of his ten-year sentence in Colorado, then returned to Canada in 2012 a free man. But a boss is never without enemies. Just before Vito's release, his son "Nick, Jr." was shot to death at the age of the age of forty-four. And just after, the 86-old patriarch Nicolò was killed by sniper in his kitchen. These circumstances paralleled curiously those of the Violi murders.

PORTO EMPEDOCLE

GIULIANO GUAZZELLI: THE MASTIFF

They called Giuliano Guazzelli "the Mastiff" for his ability to sniff out criminal networks. This colonel of the carabiniere knew the name of every gang member in Agrigento at a time the province was seeing up to eighty murders per year. In the early 1990s, the region was a viper's nest dominated by the *Stidda*, the southern homegrown version of the Mafia that had murdered his associate, Judge Rosario Livatino. Guazzelli eventually tracked down the killers and brought them to justice. Rather than retire with a pen-

As he drove the expressway, Colonel Giuliano Guazzelli was ambushed by men with Kalashnikovs: Highway SS 115 near Via Lorenzo Compatti.

sion as was his due, the fifty-nine-year-old agent signed on for more service. Guazzelli frequently received death threats but told no one. He traveled without bodyguards, making the regular commute from his home in Menfi to his office in Agrigento. On the afternoon of April 4, 1992, as the colonel drove his Fiat Ritmo homeward on the expressway passing through the city of Porto Empedocle, a Fiat minivan pulled up next to his car and forced it screeching into the guardrail. The side door was open, and three hooded men with Kalashnikovs inside fired fifty shots at their victim. Several people at an apartment building near the scene witnessed the attack. One called the police and another noted the license number of the van as it sped away, accompanied by a Renault 9. Yet another reported that one of the assailants leapt from the van and rushed to Guazzelli, who fell to his knees as the hit man finished him off with a final shot. The roundup of *stiddari* produced five convictions and four sentences, but all were later overturned. The reason for Guazzelli's death sentence was never stated, but it was implied by his high conviction rate.

FAVARA

GERLANDINO MESSINA: NUMBER TWO

So effective had Colonel Guazzelli been as a crime fighter that mafioso Gerlandino Messina had to cooperate with his enemies in

Carabiniere commandos captured fugitive boss Gerlandino Messina in this building: Via Stati Uniti, 79.

the *Stidda* to take the officer out. And Messina had good reason to despise the *Stidda*. In 1986, when Messina was thirteen, two *stiddari* peppered his father's face with buckshot, killing the boss in front of two of his other children. A few weeks later, his uncle suffered the same fate. Messina had to grow up fast during the bloody vendetta that followed—he became the de facto boss of Porto Empedocle at the tender age of fourteen. In 1999, he landed on the list of Italy's thirty most-dangerous fugitives, sought for several murders. On June 25, 2010, the other heavy of Agrigento, Giuseppe Falsone, was captured in Marseille. This arrest propelled Messina, Falsone's underboss, into the number-two slot, just below super-fugitive Matteo Messina Denaro. Then came the blitz of October 23. Exploding flash grenades announced the arrival of twenty carabiniere commandos at Messina's hideout, a rundown apartment in Favara. One team smashed through the front door while another clambered in an upstairs window. Although armed with a pair of 9mm pistols, Messina was caught unawares while playing a *Godfather*-themed Xbox game. The agents found a biography of Totò Riina and, more significantly, a list of local businesses they believed Messina had targeted for extortion. "You bastard!" shouted one of the agents. "You're the one who killed Guazzelli!" Later, a melee erupted outside the barracks that held Messina when one of his relatives attacked a gaggle of reporters. Messina's mother was there to learn whether he was still alive. "We love you!" she shouted to her homicidal son.

CANICATTÌ

SAETTA AND LIVATINO: ASSASSINS' HIGHWAY

State Highway 640 runs over the rolling expanse of bucolic countryside in Agrigento province. At night, this road is deserted, which was how Judge Antonino Saetta and his mentally impaired adult son found it shortly before 11 p.m. on September 25, 1988. As they headed homeward in a Lancia Prisma, a stolen BMW carrying four or five men zoomed up behind them. The Prisma's rear-left window exploded as two Belgian 9mm machine guns sprayed lead from the passing BMW. The judge swerved to the right and swiped the guardrail, which sent the car ricocheting across the road to a stop. The attackers pulled over and finished the assault by perforating the Prisma—forty-seven shots in all—to make sure its occupants were dead. They left Saetta slumped over the steering wheel. The arm of his blood-drenched son jutted out the opposite window. The BMW was abandoned a mile and a half away and set on fire.

Judge Saetta had always worked far from the media spotlight but he had reeled in some of the biggest fish of the era. He upheld the life sentence of Michele Greco for the Chinnici assassination and sent away the murderers of Captain Basile. It was Saetta's refusal to "bend" on the latter verdict, according to a mafioso, that sealed his fate. But the Saetta murder was also a preemptive action. The magistrate had been set to preside over the appeals process of the Mafia maxi-trials. For the double homicide of Saetta and son, life sentences were doled out to Totò Riina, Francesco Madonia and hit man Pietro Ribisi, the boss of an Agrigento crime family, who later offed himself in prison.

Two anti-Mafia magistrates of Canicattì were assassinated while driving on the same stretch of highway. Judge Antonino Saetta (above) died, with his son, in the car, while Judge Rosario Livatino was shot as he ran down an embankment. A small cult of pilgrims visits Livatino's tomb: Via Nazionale.

Like Saetta, Rosario Livatino of Canicattì was a reserved magistrate who served the state without the kind of armed protection usually lavished on the senators of Rome. The "boy judge"—he first donned the robe at twenty-six—rooted out local municipal corruption that was part of the national "Tangentopoli" bribery scandal of the 1990s. Fifteen *Stidda* members were scheduled for a sentencing hearing on the day of his death. That morning—September 21, 1990—Livatino drove his Ford Fiesta along the same stretch of Highway 640 that had been ideal for Saetta's ambushers two years earlier. Like a cruel parody of the escort he'd been refused, a white car pulled up on one side of Livatino and a motorcycle on the other. The man on the back of the bike shot him in the shoulder as the white car forced him off the road. The judge jumped out, scaled the guardrail and ran down an embankment. His pursuers followed and shot him down. The coup de grace—a bullet in the head—finished the job. It took just a month for Colonel Giuliano Guazzelli, the "Mastiff" of the carabiniere, to track Livatino's assassins to the pizzeria that employed them in Cologne, Germany. The hit turned out to be a collaboration of two *Stidda* families in Agrigento. Since then, a small cult has grown around the memory of Livatino. In a speech delivered by Pope John Paul II in 1993, the magistrate was praised as "a martyr of the law and, indirectly, also of the faith." Pilgrims visit his tomb and a beatification effort is underway.

RACALMUTO

LEONARDO SCIASCIA: SOUTHERN GOTHIC

Few writers have had as privileged a view of the Mafia as Leonardo Sciascia. The celebrated mystery novelist, playwright and essayist lived most of his life in the small town of Racalmuto. He drew from the sulphur mining region's pageant of tragicomic individuals who lived shackled by ancient codes of honor and omertà: the superstitious peasant, the cuckolded husband, the bribed politician, the Fascist sympathizer, the honest detective mocked by the savvy mafioso and foiled by his victims who conceal the boss's crimes. Sciascia's characters are portrayed with the affection of a close observer and placed into infuriating puzzles that reveal the writer's worldly, cynical intellect. With the 1961 publication of *The Day of the Owl*, Sciascia entered the Sicilian literary canon to sit alongside Luigi Pirandello, on whom he modeled his work, and Giuseppe Tomasi di Lampedusa, author of the masterpiece, *The Leopard*.

Sciascia followed his book with a panoply of works, both fiction and non-fiction: political and critical treatises, plays, essays and plenty more mysteries. He dabbled in real politics as well.

A life-size statue of author Leonardo Sciascia (left) is set where he regularly took his stroll: Via Giuseppe Garibaldi, 176. The twin graves of Sciascia and his wife lay at the entrance to the cemetery: Road SP 152.

He was elected to serve on the Palermo city council in 1975, only to resign in disgust a few years later over the "historic compromise" between his Communist party and the Christian Democrats. The 1978 kidnapping and murder of DC party head Aldo Moro by the Red Brigades inspired an angry tract from Sciascia. He reproduced the politician's letters and scrutinized connections between the terrorists, the Mafia and Prime Minister Andreotti. Inflamed by the day's political intrigues and publishing controversies, Sciascia attacked the "professionals of the anti-Mafia." The outburst, in hindsight, was seen as misplaced and ill-informed, a sentiment from a contradictory Sicilian who wrote of his home town, "I tried to recount something of the life of a place that I love, and I hope I gave a sense of how very far this life is from liberty and justice, that is, from reason."

SELECTED BIBLIOGRAPHY

A great debt is owed to the many Mafia historians whose groundbreaking research made this book possible. While I have consulted every book about the Sicilian Mafia published in English, and several more in Italian, I drew mainly from the works listed below. Additional materials included court transcripts and Italian newspapers. The writings of journalists Dino Pasternostro, Salvo Palazzolo and Rino Giacalone were invaluable.

Behan, Tom. *Defiance: The Story of One Man Who Stood Up to the Sicilian Mafia.* London: I.B. Tauris, 2008.

Bolzoni, Attilio, and Giuseppe D'Avanzo. *Il capo dei capi: vita e carriera criminale di Totò Riina.* Milan: Libri, 2007.

Bonanno, Joseph. *A Man of Honor: The Autobiography of Joseph Bonanno.* New York: Simon and Schuster, 1983.

Camilleri, Andrea. *Le Pecore e il pastore.* Palermo: Sellerio, 2007.

Catanzaro, Raimondo. *Men of Respect: A Social History of the Sicilian Mafia.* New York: The Free Press, 1988.

Chandler, Billy Jaynes. *King of the Mountain: The Life and Death of Giuliano the Bandit.* DeKalb, Illinois: Northern Illinois University Press, 1988

Ciancimino, Massimo, and Francesco La Licata. *Don Vito: The Secret Life of the Mayor of the Corleonesi.* London: Quescus, 2010.

Deaglio, Enrico. *Il raccolto rosso, 1982-2010: Cronaca di una guerra di mafia e delle sue tristissime conzeguenze.* Milan: Saggiatore, 2010.

Dickie, John. *Cosa Nostra: A History of the Sicilian Mafia.* London: Coronet Books, 2004.

Duggan, Christopher. *Fascism and the Mafia.* New Haven: Yale University Press, 1989.

Fentress, James. *Rebels and Mafiosi: Death in a Sicilian Landscape.* Ithaca: Cornell University Press, 2000.

Follain, John. *The Last Godfathers: Inside the Mafia's Most Infamous Family.* New York: Thomas Dunne Books, 2008.

Follain, John. *Vendetta: The Mafia, Judge Falcone, and the Quest for Justice.* London: Hodder & Stoughton, 2012.

Gambetta, Diego. *The Sicilian Mafia: The Business of Private Protection.* Cambridge, Massachusetts: Harvard University Press, 1993.

Lamothe, Lee, and Adrian Humphreys. *The Sixth Family: The Collapse of the New York Mafia and the Rise of Vito Rizzuto.* Mississauga, Ontario: John Wiley and Sons, 2006.

Lamothe, Lee, and Antonio Nicaso. *Bloodline: Project Omertà and the Fall of the Mafia's Royal Family.* Toronto: Harper Collins Publishers Ltd., 2001.

Lodato, Saverio. *Ho ucciso Giovanni Falcone: La confessione di Giovanni Brusca.* Milan: Mondadori, 2006.

Lodato, Saverio. *Trent'anni di mafia: Storia di una guerra inifinita.* Milan: Mondadori, 2006.

Longrigg, Clare. *Boss of Bosses: How Bernardo Provenzano Saved the Mafia.* London: John Murray, 2008.

Lupo, Salvatore. *History of the Mafia.* New York: Columbia University Press, 2009.

Marino, Giuseppe Carlo. *I padrini.* Rome: Newton Compton, 2006.

Newark, Tim. *Mafia Allies.* St. Paul: Zenith Press, 2007.

Pantaleone, Michele. *The Mafia and Politics.* New York: Coward-McCann, Inc., 1966.

Paolo, Letizia. *Mafia Brotherhoods.* New York: Oxford University Press, 2003.

Siebert, Renate. *Secrets of Life and Death: Women and the Mafia.* London: Verso, 1996.

Sterling, Claire. *Octopus: The Long Reach of the International Sicilian Mafia.* New York: Touchstone, 1990.

Stille, Alexander. *Excellent Cadavers: The Mafia and the Death of the First Italian Republic.* New York: Vintage Books, 1995.

INDEX

(Places in boldface)

Addaura 107-9
Agostino, Antonino 153-4
Aiello, Michele 84-5
Aiello, Piera 201-3
Alberti, Gerlando 19
Alcamo Marina 143-5
Almerico, Pasquale 129-31
Andreotti, Giulio 29, 31, 66, 88, 110-1, 149, 200, 232
Aprile, Andrea Finocchiaro 192
Apuzzo, Carmine 143
Arcangioli, Giovanni 38
Asta, Barbara Rizzo 213-5
Atria, Rita 201-3
Ayala, Giuseppe 38
Badalamenti, Gaetano 19, 23, 30, 61, 81, 147-9, 152
Bagarella, Calogero 54, 71, 168, 169
Bagarella, Leoluca 27, 70-2, 74, 90-2, 99-100, 125, 139, 155, 168, 170, 179
Bagarella, Ninetta 100, 169-71
Bagheria 83-5
Barbara, Joseph 143
Basile, Emanuele 29, 59-60, 101, 138-40, 229
Benedict XVI (pope) 76
Berlusconi, Silvio 57-8, 73, 93, 180
Bisacquino 181-2
Bommarito, Giuseppe 59-60
Bonanno family 23-4, 222, 226
Bonanno, Joe 23-4, 28, 141-3, 189, 225

Bongiorno, Paolo 219-20
Bontà, Paulino 65
Bontate, Giovanni 67, 77, 103
Bontate, Stefano 29, 61-2, 65-7, 76-7, 148
Bonura, Franco 64
Borgetto 136
Borghese, Junio Valerio 51
Borsellino, Paolo 8, 32, 35, 36-9, 51, 56, 72, 77, 102, 139-40, 153, 157-8, 201-2
Bosco, Giovanni 105
Brancaccio 73-6
Brusca, Bernardo 32, 59, 102, 126-7
Brusca, Giovanni 34, 58, 59-60, 125-7, 134, 155-7, 179, 180, 210
Burrafato, Antonino 90-2
Burrafato, Totò 91-2
Buscetta, Tommaso 19, 23-4, 35, 50-1, 56, 66, 80, 88, 102, 111, 148-9
Caccamo 92-4
Calò, Pippo 103
Camporeale 128-31
Cancemi, Salvatore 103, 155
Cangelosi, Calogero 129-30
Canicattì 229-31
Capaci 154-8
Capone, Al 54
Carnevale, Corrado 36, 81-2, 111
Carnevale, Salvatore 96-8
Caruana, Alfonso 222
Caruana, Carmelo 221-2
Caruana-Cuntrera family 221-2, 225
Casarrubea, Giuseppe 135
Cascio Ferro, Vito 22-3, 41, 181-2, 189
Cassarà, Ninni 32, 78, 86-7, 100-2, 195-6
Castellammare del Golfo 141-3
Castellano, Paul 187
Castelvetrano 203-7
Castronovo, Stefano 76-7
Cattolica Eraclea 223-6
Cavataio, Michele 54, 80
Chinnici, Rocco 32-5, 101, 229
Ciaccio Montalto, Giangiacomo 211-2
Ciaculli 78-82
Ciancimino, Massimo 57-8, 67, 108-9
Ciancimino, Vito 47, 55-8, 61, 81, 83-4, 88, 90, 109, 110, 168
Cinà, Antonino 56, 64
Cinisi 147-51

Conticello, Vincenzo 44
Contrada, Bruno 67, 102
Coppola, Agostino 99
Corleone 161-77
Costa, Gaetano 29-30, 61-2, 78
Cotroni family 225
Cotroni, Vic 225
Crispi, Francesco 162, 184
Cristina, Cosimo 40, 89-90
Croceverde 78-82
Cuccia, Ciccio 121-2
Cuffaro, Salvatore "Totò" 84-5, 200
D'Aleo, Mario 59-60
D'Alì, Antonio 207
Dalla Chiesa, Carlo Alberto 30-2, 33, 101, 167, 178
De Donno, Giuseppe 39, 56, 58
De Maria, Gregorio 204-5
De Mauro, Mauro 27, 40, 46, 50-1, 66
Dell'Utri, Marcello 39, 57-8, 180
Di Cristina, Giuseppe 51, 61-2
Di Maggio, Balduccio 88
Di Matteo, Giuseppe, 72, 125-7
Di Matteo, Santino 125-7
Di Pisa, Calcedonio 79
Di Salvo, Rosario 49
Dolci, Danilo 145-7
Domino, Claudio 102-3
Falcetta, Salvatore 143
Falcone, Giovanni 8, 32-3, 34-7, 39, 51, 56, 70, 72, 78, 92-3, 101-2, 107-8, 125, 154-8, 195
Falsone, Giuseppe 228
Favara 227-8
Ferdinand III (king) 9, 17, 177-8
Ferranti, Vincenzo 128-9
Ficuzza 177-9
Filippi, Ernesto Eugenio 128
Florio family 39, 95
Fontana, Giuseppe 95-6
Francese, Mario 99-100
Galante, Carmine 23
Galatolo, Angelo
Gambino family 27, 61-2, 63, 65, 222
Gambino, Carlo 186-7
Ganci, Calogero 60
Garibaldi, Giuseppe 9, 68
Gariffo, Carmelo 173, 175
Genco Russo, Giuseppe 23, 40, 147, 193-5
Genovese, Vito 190, 194
Gentile, Nick 221
Geraci, Mico 93-4

Geraci, Nenè 133-4
Giaccone, Paolo 69-70, 86
Giacomelli, Alberto 208-9
Giammarinaro, Pino 200-1
Giammona, Antonino 20-1
Giardinello 113-5
Giuffrè, Nino 84, 93-4
Giuliano, Boris 26-7, 32, 34, 71, 101, 138-9
Giuliano, Salvatore 5, 90, 115-20, 123-4, 135-8, 203-5
Grassi, Libero 41-4
Graviano, Filippo 71, 72-3, 76
Graviano, Giuseppe 71, 72-3, 76
Greco, Michele 32-3, 72, 78-82, 86-7, 103, 195, 229
Greco, Pino 31, 46, 62, 67, 71, 81, 86-7, 92, 102, 179, 195-6
Greco, Salvatore 54, 78-80
Grigoli, Salvatore 76
Guajana, Rodolfo 44
Guazzelli, Giuliano 226-7, 231
Gullo, Fausto 96, 217
Gurreri, Rosario 224
Ienna, Gianni 73
Ievolella, Vito 47-8
Ilardo, Gino 179-80
Impastato, Giuseppe 149-51
Intile, Francesco 84
Inzerillo family 29, 61-3, 66, 115, 155
Inzerillo, Giovanni 63
Inzerillo, Salvatore "Totuccio" 30, 61-3, 65-7, 105, 196
John Paul II (pope) 75, 231
La Barbera, Angelo 79-80, 110
La Barbera, Salvatore 79-80, 110
La Torre, Pio 30, 47, 48-9
Lansky, Meyer 187
Leggio, Luciano 25-7, 40, 46, 52, 71, 76, 81, 139, 148, 163-8, 169, 172
Lercara Friddi 186-8
Li Causi, Girolamo 124, 192
Liga, Giuseppe, 104
Lima, Salvo 51, 56, 66, 81, 88, 109-11
Livatino, Rosario 226, 230-1
Lo Bue, Giuseppe 173-5
Lo Piccolo, Salvatore 43, 63-4, 67, 104, 105, 113-5, 206
Lo Piccolo, Sandro 63-4, 67, 113-5
Lo Presti, Gaetano 68
Locogrande 208-9
Lucca Sicula 219-20
Luciano, Charles "Lucky" 23-4, 141-2, 163, 186-8, 194,

221

Madonia, Francesco 102, 229
Madonia, Nino 34
Madonia, Piddu 179-80
Mancino, Nicola 39
Mancuso, Giuseppe 208
Mancuso, Lenin 26
Mandela, Rosario 119
Mangano, Angelo 76, 89-90
Maniaci, Pino 134
Manno, Antonino 223-4
Maniaci, Pino 134
Manzella, Cesare 79, 147, 149, 151
Maranzano, Salvatore 141-2
Marchese, Filippo 62, 68-70
Marchese, Giuseppe 19, 69
Marchese, Nino 92
Marino, Salvatore 87, 101
Marino Mannoia, Francesco 60, 65-6, 91
Masseria, Joe 141-2
Mattarella, Bernardo 28-9, 55
Mattarella, Piersanti 28-9
Mattei, Enrico 51
Mazara del Vallo 207-8
Mazzara, Vito 211
Messina Denaro, Francesco 205, 207
Messina Denaro, Matteo 67, 71, 134, 205-7, 210, 228

Messina, Gerlandino 227-8
Mezzojuso 179-80
Miceli, Salvatore 200-1
Minasola, Netto 137
Minore family 212
Miraglia, Accursio 217-9, 220
Mondello 109-11
Monreale 137-40
Montagna, Salvatore 143
Montalto, Giuseppe 209-11
Montalto, Salvatore 195-6
Montana, Beppe 33, 86-7, 100-1, 195
Montelepre 115-9
Morello, Giuseppe 22, 181
Mori, Cesare 122, 182, 188-90
Mori, Mario 39, 56, 57-8, 180
Morici, Pietro 59-60
Moro, Aldo 150-1, 232
Morvillo, Francesca 155-7
Mussolini, Benito 39, 48, 121-2, 166, 182, 188-90
Mussomeli 193-5
Mutolo, Gaspare 60, 111
Napola 210-11
Navarra, Michele 52, 163-8, 177, 218
Nicastro, Vito 207
Nicchi, Gianni 63-4, 67
Notarbartolo, Emanuele 94-6
Obinu, Mauro 180

Olino, Renato 144-5
Palazzolo, Saveria Benedetta 173-6
Palermo 15-78, 99-105
Palermo, Carlo 213-5
Palizzolo, Raffaele 95-6
Palma 209-11
Panepinto, Lorenzo 183-4
Pantaleone, Michele 189-90, 190-2
Panzeca, Peppino 92-4
Pappalardo, Salvatore 75
Partanna 201-3
Partinico 133-7
Pecorelli, Mino 148
Peruzzo, Giovanni Battista 185-6
Petrosino, Joe 21-3, 181
Piana degli Albanesi 121-2
Piazza, Emanuele 154
Pirandello, Luigi 39, 231
Pisciotta, Gaspare 46, 118-9, 124, 138, 204-5
Pizzolungo 213-5
Polizzello 192-3
Portella della Ginestra 122-4
Porticello 86-7
Porto Empedocle 226-7
Prestifilippo, Mario 86-7, 195-6
Provenzano, Angelo 173

Provenzano, Bernardo 5, 25, 32, 54, 55-6, 63-4, 83-4, 85, 93-4, 105, 109, 113, 115, 133-4, 168, 172-6, 179, 206
Puccio, Vincenzo 140, 179-80
Puglisi, Giuseppe "Pino" 73-6
Racalmuto 231-2
Raccuglia, Mimmo 206
Riccio, Michele 179-80
Riccobono, Rosario 81, 114
Riina, Gaetano 207, 208-9
Riina, Giovanni 170-1
Riina, Salvatore "Salvuccio" 68, 170-1
Riina, Salvatore "Totò" 19, 25, 32-3, 46, 49, 51-3, 54, 56, 58, 61-3, 66, 69-70, 71, 72, 81, 83-4, 88, 90, 100, 105, 109, 133-4, 139, 155, 157, 168-71, 172, 178-9, 196, 209, 228-9
Rizzotto, Placido 166-8, 177
Rizzuto, Nicolò "Nick" 224-6
Rizzuto, Nicolò "Nick, Jr." 226
Rizzuto, Vito 226
Roccapalumba 188-90
Roosevelt, Theodore 23
Rosi, Francesco 27, 204
Rostagno, Mauro 210-11
Rotolo, Nino 63-4, 115
Ruffini, Ernesto 147

Russo, Giuseppe 144-5, 177-9
Sacco, Vanni 128-31
Saetta, Antonino
Sagana 119-20
Salemi 199-201
Salvo, Ignazio 51, 66, 87-8, 111, 200
Salvo, Nino 66, 87-8, 111, 200
San Cipirello 125-7
San Giuseppe Jato 125-7
Santa Flavia 87-8
Santapaola, Nitto 83-4, 209
Santo Stefano Quisquina 183-6
Scaglione, Pietro 45-7
Schifani, Rosario Costa 157
Sciacca 217-9
Sciara 94-8
Sciascia, Leonardo 40, 231-2
Settecasi, Giuseppe 221
Sgarbi, Vittorio 199-201
Sgroi, Paolo 115
Siculiana 221-2
Siegel, Bugsy 187
Sinagra, Vincenzo 69-70
Sinatra, Frank 186-8
Sindona, Michele 27, 66
Spadaro, Tommaso 47-8, 86
Spagnolo, Giuseppe 223-4
Spampinato, Giovanni 40
Spatola, Rosario 29, 61
Spatuzza, Gaspare 39, 72-3, 76
Sutera 195-6
Termini Imerese 89-90
Terranova, Cesare 24-7, 28, 32, 34, 48, 101
Terrasini 152-3
Tomasi di Lampedusa, Giuseppe 231
Torretta, Pietro 19
Toscani, Oliviero 200
Trapani 211-3
Trappeto 145-7
Triolo, Ugo 171-2
Turrisi Colonna, Nicolò 20-1
Valderice 211
Verga, Giovanni 39
Verro, Bernardino 161-3, 177, 183
Vesco, Giuseppe 144-5
Villagrazia di Carini 153-4
Villalba 190-2
Violi, Paolo 225
Virga, Vincenzo 209, 211
Vitale, Giusy 134-5
Vitale, Leonardo 133-5
Vitale, Vito 133-4
Vizzini, Calogero 65, 120, 190-2, 193-4
Zucchetto, Calogero 32-3, 86, 195-6